The Art of
Contempor
American
Pottery

Published by

**krause
publications**

700 East State Street • Iola, WI 54990-0001
715/445-2214 • FAX: 715/445-4087   www.krause.com

Please call or write us for our free catalog. To place an order or to receive our catalog, call 800-258-0929 or use our regular business telephone at 715-445-2214.

Library of Congress Catalog Number: 2001088593

ISBN: 0-87341-906-5

Printed in the United States of America

COVER PHOTO
Elizabeth Lurie: "Soy Bottle," porcelain, 6" x 3", thrown and altered, hand built, C. 9.5.
Photo by Neil Lurie

Matthew Metz: "Covered Jar," Porcelain, 7" x 5.25", thrown, altered excised, salt fired, C. 10. Photo by Dan Meyers. Collection of the author.

"I'm interested in form, function and line. Making and using tableware allows me to look and learn from my pots and the pots of others."

Anne Fallis Elliott

"Brown Lidded Jar," stoneware, 6.5" x 4.5", wheel thrown, sash glazed, C. 8. Photo by Kevin Noble.

For my mother:
a journalist at heart

Acknowledgments

I owe a debt of gratitude to all those potters who made the effort to supply me with the images and information found within these pages. Were it not for space limitations, many more potters might have been included in this survey. Perhaps a future publication will provide what could not be included here. I would also like to thank the potters' galleries for providing their contact information. This is an essential contribution for those who may be inspired to acquire this wonderful work.

I extend my appreciation to Carrie Jacobsen, Louise Harter and Sheila Hoffman for patiently and wisely pointing out some of the more glaring defects in the early drafts of this effort. Each was instrumental in providing needed feedback and criticism. In addition, Robin Hopper and Phyllis Blair Clark were instrumental in providing information that led me to numerous potters now represented in this book.

Thanks also to Marty Amt, for introducing me to Linda Crocker Simmons. She allowed me to scrutinize her late husband's extensive and wonderful collection of pottery, including the examples of Leach and Hamada shown in Chapter 7. That was truly a fortuitous and enjoyable meeting for which I am grateful.

Also, Krause Publications deserves recognition for taking a chance on this novice writer and having the insight to consider the topic worthwhile and deserving attention.

In addition, I would also like to thank Montgomery College, Rockville, Maryland for providing a sabbatical and release time to work on this project. The sabbatical paved the way for the primary effort and for this I am indebted and grateful.

Finally, I am extremely thankful for the continued and unflagging support and love of my children, Kendra and Mathew, and especially my wife, Margaret. Without her confidence, encouragement, and faith in me, this book would never have come into being.

"Clay is molded
to make a vessel,
but the utility of the vessel
lies in
the space
where there is nothing....
Thus,
taking advantage of
what is,
we recognize the utility of
what is not."

Lao Tzu

Connie Christensen: "Covered Jar,"
porcelain, 8" x 5", thrown, wood
fired, C. 10. Photo by John Bonath.

Contents

Warren MacKenzie: "Teapot," stoneware, 4.5" x 8" x 5", thrown and assembled. Photo by Dan Meyers. Collection of the author.

Foreword

Useful objects are almost always praised in a backhanded way. You can read critics saying that such-and-such a thing is compelling in spite of it being an object made for some mundane use.

And how often have you heard someone who is buying a piece of pottery say, "Of course this is too good to use"? At best use is seen as simplistic, a given that holds no mystery or value, sometimes even an impediment to artistic expression. While it is true that we all understand use—that is we all know what to do with a cup containing tea—it does not mean that an artist can't employ use as part of a larger aesthetic proposition. Sight, for example, is something that, most of us at least, also take for granted. That does not mean, however, that just because painting is understood through that faculty, it is mundane. Sight is merely the path that painting uses to communicate feelings and ideas.

If we view use in the same way then it is possible to see its potential as an avenue through which an artist is able to present a particular set of concerns to an audience. A useful object addresses not only the retina, but all the senses and can layer its information in such a complex manner that meanings can be present on numerous levels.

The question then arises, can touch, smell and taste as well as sight and hearing carry the kind of information and feeling that form the profound, life-altering experiences that we expect from great art?

The American philosopher John Dewey argued in 1932 in his collection of essays titled *Art As Experience* that, "There is no limit to the capacity of immediate sensuous experience to absorb into itself meanings and values that in and of themselves—that is in the abstract—would be designated 'ideal' and 'spiritual'…Nothing that a man has ever reached by the highest flight of thought or penetrated by any probing insight is inherently such that it may not become the heart and core of sense."

Potters and lovers of pottery know, on an intuitive level, this to be true because great pottery of the past has literally changed their lives. They have experienced, in its presence, that transcendental moment that occurs whenever one is confronted by great art.

There are two important questions, though, that I think potters and craftspeople in general need to ask themselves if they are going to make work that will give us the kind of intense pleasure and sense of wonderment which that early work continues to provide. The first is: What is the purpose of useful handmade objects in the twenty-first century? The second is: What is the role of use in realizing this goal?

Kevin Hluch's *The Art of Contemporary American Pottery* points us in the right direction. He examines aspects of use where the possibility exists for potters to express their deepest concerns about what it means to be human in this modern information age. This challenge, to create useful pottery that expands our awareness and causes us change the way we look at the world around us, is one that I hope American potters will accept.

—Rob Barnard

Messenger of Art

*P*ottery is pure art; it is art freed from any imitative intention. Sculpture, to which it is most nearly related, had from
the first an imitative intention, and is perhaps to that extent
less free for the expression of the will to form than pottery; pottery is plastic art in its most abstract essence.[1]

Herbert Read

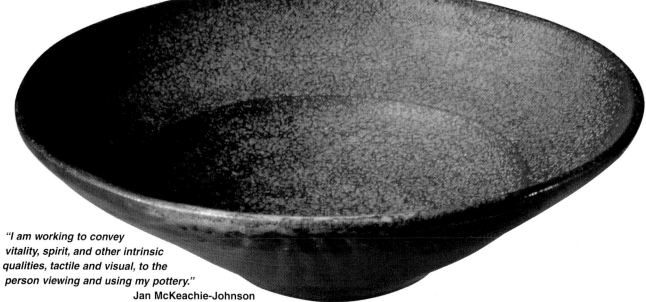

**"I am working to convey
vitality, spirit, and other intrinsic
qualities, tactile and visual, to the
person viewing and using my pottery."**
Jan McKeachie-Johnson

"Bowl," stoneware, 4.5" x 14", thrown, wood fired, C. 10.
Photo by Peter Lee.

Pottery is a distinctive form of artistic expression that possesses unique utilitarian attributes. In
contrast, contemporary art is generally accepted as
being occupied with purely aesthetic concerns.
Potters are unique artists in the sense they are concerned not only with aesthetic issues, but also with
utility.

Perceptions of what constitutes art have dramatically changed over time. And while a discussion
of contemporary art can elicit confusing and sometimes unintelligible jargon, it is possible to produce
at least a few coherent statements on this subject.
To put pottery in a contemporary context it may be

best to define a few crucial terms at the outset. And
it seems appropriate to begin at a fundamental
level.

A common dictionary definition of art is this:
The conscious production or arrangement of
sounds, colors, forms, movements, or other elements in a manner that affects the sense of beauty.

Pottery historically has been considered a craft
activity, so it's best to note its definition as well: An
occupation or trade requiring manual dexterity or
skilled artistry.

Alas, since beauty is integral to the definition of
art it is advisable to note a commonly accepted

"My investigation is a search for beauty."
Alleghany Meadows

"Sauce Boat," porcelain, 6" x 7" x 5", wheel thrown, altered, salt-fired, C. 9. Photo by the artist.

meaning of this term as well: Beauty is that which pleases the senses and exalts the mind.

Finally then, a beautiful pot can be considered a skillfully made utilitarian object incorporating a selection of forms, textures, colors, etc., which delight the senses and elevate the mind.

But things are not so simple.

One big problem is that contemporary artists do not universally share the definition of beauty. In fact, many artists today often create objects disassociated from the concept of beauty.

Since beauty can only be broadly defined, it is in the particulars where the discussion becomes tortured. For example, some people may contend that there is no difference between something "ugly" and something "beautiful." However, can that which is ugly or grotesque be pleasing to the senses or uplifting to the spirit? Without doubt, ugly

"The essence of my work lies in the contrast between simple and articulate ceramic forms and spirited, free-hand treatment of the surfaces."
Kathy Erteman

"Tea for Two," white ware, 5" x 1" x 3", slip cast and hand built with carving, C. 2. Photo by D. James Dee.

things are neither pleasing nor inspiring. Thus, they cannot be beautiful. And certainly it is only humans that can distinguish between the two.

Furthermore, even beautiful things are at times unsettling or vexatious, and some may contend that what is beautiful to one may be ugly to another. Oddly, it may even appear that some of one blends into the other. It is in this sense the Japanese philosopher Soetsu Yanagi has observed, "All true art has, somewhere, an element of the grotesque."[2] In other words, beautiful art expressions have within them a secondary but essential component of their opposing character.

Often, it is the dominance of one characteristic versus its contrasting element that determines the conclusion. A judgment of beauty, it appears, is not simply the resolution of an aesthetic ideal but is a struggle to bring oppositional forms into balance in a unique, pleasing and uplifting fashion.

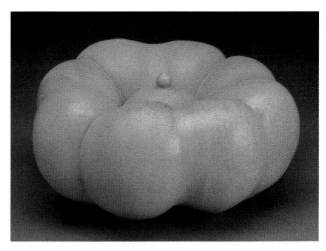

"I am interested in the way planes and parts move, shift, merge and meet one another, and the order that grows out of this interaction."
Erica Wurtz

"Roll Jar," stoneware, 6" x 12" x 12", thrown and hand built, C. 9. Photo by John Polak.

For this, freedom is essential for the artist. However, unlike contemporary artists who are indifferent to utilitarian values, the freedom to creatively pursue unique forms presents pitfalls to the potter. For example, if the pursuit of novel technique or form negates the utility of a pot, then the object sacrifices one of its qualifying values: utility.

In this sense, there is a built-in contradiction, philosophically, between the intent of the utilitarian potter and the sculptor. The potter strives to make art that will co-exist benevolently, admirably and beautifully in the domestic environment. On the other hand, complex, three-dimensional forms may be fine for the sculptor but may simultaneously limit the utility of a pottery form. And, since the beauty of pottery is often judged by the hand, these more aggressive versions of pottery may not be successful pots.

Artists make objects where the visual attributes alone determine evocative qualities, not elements of touch or elements of use.

There are some who would trim the role of function from utilitarian pottery to acquire enhanced respect or prestige that currently exists in the fine art culture for non-utilitarian art objects. But this diminishes the distinct and valuable service pottery performs and obfuscates its original histori-cal role in societies.

As Wayne Higby, professor of ceramic art at Alfred University has observed, "Simply stated, the

"My aim is to combine the traditional functional shapes and colorful, high quality glazes into pottery that is safe, durable and at the same time bringing beauty and enjoyment into any dining situation."

Dale Neese

"Stoneware Teapot," stoneware, 6" x 6", wheel thrown, C. 10. Photo by Ansen Seale.

"My objective is to make a good, honest pot that inspires the user to reach for it every day."

Meg Dickerson

"Teapot," white stoneware, 6.5" x 7.25" x 4.5", wheel thrown, C. 6. Photo by artist.

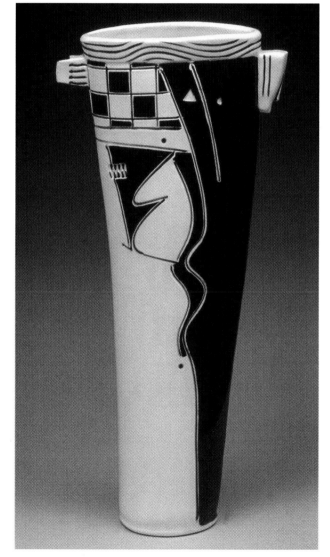

"Even though I am compulsive and process-oriented toward clay as a raw material, I remain devoted to the concept of painting and it is a defining element in my work."

Tom Schiller

"Pocket Vase," white earthenware, 15" x 7.5" x 3", slab construc-tion, underglaze painting, C. 04. Photo by Janet Ryan.

teapot must 'work' or be relegated to the shelf. One sure test of quality for a functional pot is whether or not it can be used."[3] This element of usefulness is an essential aspect of the beauty of pottery.

There are, of course, conceptual teapots intend-ed for aesthetic contemplation only. But these forms are relegated to the shelf or sculpture pedestal, to be admired only at a distance.

And while it is true that pottery possesses sculp-tural attributes such as volume, depth, positive and negative space, shape and richness of surface, pot-tery is not, and can never be, sculpture.

Certainly, successful pottery must also be made by a crafts person who knows how to make good pots. This may seem obvious but these days, it is not. Skilled artistry is required since a badly made pot will please few people. For that matter an ugly pot, poorly made, fails twice.

The ancient Greeks knew how to make pots well. At that time the term for art was "techne," or, as writer and ethnologist Ellen Dissanayake defines it, "The capacity to make or do something with a correct understanding of the principle involved." Furthermore, she states, "As in non-Western societies today, the arts were judged and appraised for their level of craftsmanship, their 'correctness' of execution, and their appropriateness."[4] This orientation is certainly much closer to today's definition of craft, not art. Useful pots lie within this fold.

Master potters invest years developing an uncanny level of exactitude in their work. As if by magic, they effortlessly bring forth unique expressive forms. The experienced potter's gestures are fluid, sure, economical—almost nonchalant in character. They are, as a result of disciplined practice, second nature.

This however, is not enough. The notion that skill alone can produce aesthetically successful pottery is, unfortunately, incorrect. An artist preoccupied solely with demonstrating exceptional technique, sadly, can produce excruciatingly lifeless work.

English potter Michael Cardew speaks incisively of this when he says, "And this is something of a paradox, because, in becoming more skillful and more expert, you think you should be making pots more successfully and more safely, but as soon as you rest content with being safe and successful, your pots begin to be static and begin to be dead. They will only stay alive if they are always being brought to birth dangerously."[5]

Like the inherent risks associated with living an unabridged life, the process of making pots must also push the edges of the known.

Pots must function without spilling, dripping, burning, scraping, cutting or otherwise offending the user. This grace in use is an essential element of the aesthetic of pottery. The aesthetic judgment of a pot is, after all, a judgment borne by the hands.

In addition, the ability of the clay to accept the gesture of the artist has always been an essential aspect of the expressive potential of art in pottery making. Both "sculptural" and "painterly" qualities can be united in pottery form.

The pot's three-dimensional pliant surface has been the canvas for artistic expression since time immemorial. Ancient pots produced in practically every settled culture around the world exhibit this obvious unquenchable need for two-dimensional expression.

In the earliest prehistoric cultures, pattern making was the expressive core of most pottery decoration. Doubtless the abstract, geometrical shapes, patterns, and designs on ancient pots had significance for the people who made them, but today we often interpret these unintelligible patterns simply as beautiful designs.

"I believe that every successful work of art reflects an intelligent and enlightened combination of imaginative ideas with highly developed skills and craftsmanship."

Val Cushing

"Soup Tureen," stoneware, 14" x 10.5", wheel thrown with hollow-thrown handles, C. 9. Photo by Brian Oglesbe.

"The structuring and proportioning of the pots' form are the areas for which my intuition is triggered; the areas for which I have the deepest feeling."

Michael Simon

"Horse Jar," stoneware, 14" x 14", wheel thrown, wax resist, salt fired, C. 8+. Photo by Walker Montgomery.

Might it be possible the pleasure derived from these patterns was a contributory reason for their creation in the first place? While not thought of as a particularly significant aesthetic undertaking today, pattern making is a viable and intriguing method of acquiring visual interest and meaning.

In his book *The Unknown Craftsman*, Soetsu Yanagi states: "To divine the significance of pattern is the same as to understand beauty itself... The relationship between beauty in the crafts and pattern is particularly profound." Pattern was a hallmark of the surface decoration of historical pottery and we see the magical presence of pattern in contemporary pottery.

"I most love to make functional objects that are used in everyday life, with pattern and subtle color to enhance the users' experience."

Robbie Lobell

"Platter," white stoneware, wheel thrown, black slip, soda fired, C. 6-8. Photo by Jim Ushkirnis.

"I am striving for generous forms to suggest that the pots both contain and offer their contents, and for lush surfaces which I hope, invite touch and use."

Sarah Jaeger

"Casserole," porcelain, 8" x 11" x 9", wheel thrown, wax resist, C. 10. Photo by Marc Digeros.

Pattern making fell out of favor for fine artists when the ability to paint an illusionistic three-dimensional image on a flat surface became the most important aesthetic goal of the Renaissance. The rise of representational painting as the "sine qua non" of artistic expression was instrumental in the elevation of certain expressive media over others. Artists struggling with the technical problems of representational painting were the heroes of the day. This bias can

still be seen in the training of artists and in the offerings of art history courses in universities and colleges today.

In addition, the idea of appropriate or preferential media has hamstrung thinking about what constitutes art today. Since the Renaissance, fine art expressions have traditionally been classified—until the 1960s, that is—as painting, sculpture, and architecture. And these expressive forms were accomplished with traditional media. Painting, for the

"I am interested in the way pattern and color can create movement on the surface of a pot and in the idea of the whole being greater than the sum of its parts."

Judy Kogod

"Rice Bowl Platter," earthenware, 18" diameter, thrown, cut lip, slips and glaze, C. 06. Photo by PRS Associates.

most part, was oil, tempera, watercolor, and gouache. Sculpture was hewn of stone or wood, or fabricated or cast from various metals.

But media proscriptions for artists began to dissolve early in the twentieth century with the impressionists. Paul Gauguin experimented with ceramics; Matisse used colored paper; Chagall made pots; and Picasso and others added newsprint, sand, and other materials to their art. As Africans had done for centuries, Europeans were suddenly free to use diverse and non-traditional media in their artistic expressions.

But even as these media restrictions were fading, the rules regarding utility continued. From the '70s onward, even though fine-art objects could be fabricated from all manner of unique and non-traditional materials, "fine art" could not be utilitarian.

However, the exclusion of this aspect of artistic expression is as specious as the arbitrary exclusion of one media at the expense of another.

Located in museums around the world are countless objects of art that incorporate utilitarian values. They include armor, stone containers, porticoes, clothing, boats, sarcophagi, weapons, jewelry, stained-glass windows, tools, toys, storage vessels,

doorways, and, of course, the ubiquitous ceramic pot. The entire hoard of art found in the tomb of Egypt's Pharaoh Tutankhamen was comprised of utilitarian objects meant for use—use in the afterlife. These items speak the language of both art and craft.

Contemporary fine-art dogma no longer emphasizes "appropriate" media, and the proclivity to excise utilitarian elements from art expressions certainly reflects a waning bias on the part of the art world in the West.

But the effect of these fabrications has been long lasting and detrimental. Potters have had to struggle against being classified as merely artisans or crafts persons rather than artists.

Compared to ancient times, few potters ply their trade today. Since the industrial revolution, mass-production techniques have become the primary means by which pottery is made. Today, machine-made pottery is both abundant and cheap. But, because of the industrial process, the individual craft person's mark was lost.

Much of the antagonism over the "art" and "craft" is about perceptions of value as it relates to both media and expressive intent.

"I feel machines can make pots faster and more economical than I, what I strive for in my pots, is to give what the machine cannot, the mark of the human hand."
Donn Buchfinck

"Cup," porcelain, 3" x 4", thrown and altered, C. 10. Photo by Gary Sutton.

"Use, which separates pottery from sculpture, makes pottery accessible and allows the viewer to actively participate in the aesthetic equation rather than being merely a passive observer."
Rob Barnard

"Covered Jar," stoneware, 7" x 6", wood fired with natural ash glaze, C. 12. Photo by Hubert Gentry.

It appears the choice for the twentieth-century potter has been this: Produce ceramic art for a high-end marketplace where utility is shunned and high prices are sought, or produce lower-priced utilitarian pottery associated with a dying folk-art tradition. The first choice strips pottery from its utilitarian roots, while with the second choice comes the loss of prestige and status normally associated with artists' creations. Neither choice is satisfactory.

Thankfully, a third choice has been presented—the studio potter. The college- or university-educated studio potter, guided in spirit by folk art and some of the practices that were the impetus of much of the historical pottery, is practically the sole originator of handmade pottery today. Against all odds, and certainly not in a traditional sense, creative, unique utilitarian pottery continues to be made today.

Critic and writer Philip Rawson has noted pottery's unique place in the pantheon of artistic expressions: "One of the prime reasons why ceramics is such an interesting art is that it fills the gap which now yawns between art and life."[6] Certainly this gap is wider today that it has ever been since handmade pottery is no longer commonplace as it was prior to the industrial revolution.

"Tableware by nature tends to be positive in attitude. I want the work to have strong forms and cheerful, spontaneous surfaces that engage the viewer over repeated readings."
Linda Arbuckle

"Square Bowl: Fall," terracotta, 8" sq. x 5", thrown and altered, majolica glaze, C. 04. Photo by the artist.

Pottery making is at once a noble, worthwhile, and daunting undertaking. Thankfully, there are studio potters today who still address those ancient values and forms to create wondrous works that inspire, endear, and encourage the passing of the day in a civilized manner.

"With these pots I hope to convey the generosity of a welcoming host, the piquancy of good and clever company, and the abundance of the plentiful well-prepared meal."
Louise Harter

"Pair of Small Cups," local stoneware, 3" x 3" x 2 1/2", wheel thrown, salt and soda fired, C. 10. Photo by Tom Mills.

1   Read, Herbert, *The Meaning of Art*, p. 41-42

2   Yanagi, Soetsu, *The Unknown Craftsman,* p. 119.

3   Higby, Wayne, *Ceramics Monthly,* 'Useful Pottery', p. 52.

4   Dissanayake, Ellen, *What is Art For?* p. 35-36.

5   Clark, Garth, *Ceramics: Comment and Review*, p. 102

6   Rawson, Phillip, *Ceramics,* p. 68.

Zen Origins

*R*epetition and contrast, symmetry and asymmetry, major and minor, dark against light, convex and concave—these and many other dualism have to be resolved in every pot by the catalytic effect of neutrals.[1]

Bernard Leach

"I am looking to express that moment when inhalation ceases and exhalation has not yet begun, that instant of complete fullness."
Robbie Lobell

"Covered Bowl," white stoneware, wheel thrown and altered, black slip, C. 6-8. Photo by artist.

To appreciate a work of art is not a particularly difficult undertaking. Indeed, the successful work of art appears to be full of "life." Somehow, magically, the essence of the maker appears infused in the expression.

Understanding how and why art conveys such an irreducible but wonderful effect is a formidable challenge. For this reason most shy away from the task or trot out the stale bromide, "Art is in the eye of the beholder."

Discussing visual art is difficult primarily because artists use a plastic language to convey emotions and ideas. Artists use lines, shapes, colors, patterns, textures and images as their alphabet. This makes for profound difficulties in *saying* why there is such insightful meaning in these expressions.

Additionally, to say an artwork is "high quality" or "good," unfortunately, describes very little. And many of the banalities offered today mask a difficult matter either ignored or avoided: Art is about the creation of beauty. Notwithstanding the discussions presented by many modern day philosophers and critics, this concept has always been and continues to be a cardinal motivating force for artists. Beauty is all around us and the plea of Japanese philosopher Soetsu Yanagi is still relevant: "I wish that everyone would realize that until recently beauty in things was commonplace and that is our responsi-

"I am interested in the relationship between qualities that the various stages of making can bring to a pot...I enjoy exploring the possibilities of contrast and unity in regard to these qualities."

Todd Wahlstrom

"Storage Jar," porcelain, 7.5" x 10", thrown, slip decorated, C.10. Photo by artist.

"I am interested in how pots can be used every day to bring art into our lives, enhancing our experience with food, adorning our homes, and providing a necessary ritual to nourish our soul and mind as well as our bodies."

Josh DeWeese

"Teabowl," stoneware, 6" x5.5", wheel thrown, wood-fired, C. 10. Photo by artist.

bility to demand that of the future."[2] Fortunately, there are many potters today who still subscribe to this important principle.

However, there will never be a conclusion regarding the essence of art expressions, even beautiful ones. Bewilderment manifested in discussions about the word "beauty" bears this out. In the end it is only the voice empowered in the artwork itself that remains. The speaker will inevitably pass away.

But it can be affirmed that an aesthetically successful pot is a utensil satisfying life-sustaining needs with an element of its creator's character ever present. In recognizing this one can see that using pottery is a daily communion and a celebration of life. This spirit is first given freely in the creation of the pot and then again in the daily activities that literally sustain and celebrate life.

And in celebrating life it may be useful to suggest what that signifies. It means imbuing the artwork with a strength of feeling that is undeniable, authentic and sincere. It means creating a work of art that is as rich and varied as the tapestry of life

itself. It means emphasizing the positive elements of life brought to us each day. It also means recognizing the chaos present in the world can also be a source of inspired healing and transformation.

A hint about the wellspring of art in general and pottery in particular can be discerned in the way artists describe their own work:

Posey Bacopoulos: "My goal is to integrate form, function and surface that brings a sense of balance and excitement to my work." Kathryn Finnerty: "I strive for a balance between the visual dialogue in a piece and the notion of usefulness." George Bowes: "Placing images on opposing sides of a form presents the opportunity to compare and contrast quite naturally. This act of comparing is something we do continually to clarify our positions on a vast array of topics."

Not surprisingly, artists often speak of contrasts, complements and oppositional elements.

This may be so since it appears our world is bound in fundamental contrasts: hot/cold, smooth/rough, straight/curved, black/white, posi-

"Contrasts and interactions are manifested through the tension that exists between the exterior and interior space, or between the texture and glaze surface of a pot."

Sam Clarkson

"Dualie, Nesting Oil and Vinegar Set," porcelain, 6" high, wheel thrown and assembled, C. 9. Photo by artist.

"Strength lies in the fluidity of opposites — of line and mass, contraction and relaxation, tension and softness, push and pull."

Jess Parker

"Oil and Vinegar Cruets," porcelain, 9" x 9", wheel thrown, soda-fired, C. 10. Photo by artist.

tive/negative, life/death, earth/sky, rational/intuitive, top/bottom, male/female, beautiful/ugly, etc. These dualistic elements, not surprisingly, also subsequently appear both as a kind of underlying and overt fabric in art expressions.

For example, a pot has both inside and outside, it can be round or square, open or closed, maladroit or elegant. And, in fact, pottery often manifests a wonderful and unique fusion of contrasting elements. It can be a combination of coarse and

"Pots can create a world of slow time where meaning can be found."

Chris Staley

"Dinner Plates," stoneware, 10" diameter, wheel thrown, C. 9. Photo by artist.

smooth textures. A pot can be very simple in form but have complex surface decoration. A plethora of elements, individually static but dynamic in combination, create a tension which often appears to constitute aesthetic success.

English potter Michael Cardew observed this when he said, "Good design in pottery is the product of a tension or 'dialectic' between the demands of pure utility and those of pure beauty, and only a long experience and continual struggle enable you to achieve a successful fusion of the two."[3]

Of course, the initial idea or feeling inspiring the expression is the organizing theme around which these dualistic elements may be arranged. And no matter what the individual's specific expressive intent, skill in its execution is a necessary qualitative determinate.

This dualistic orientation to reality, as many know, can be seen in the practice of Zen Buddhism. Presumably, the goal of enlightenment is to eliminate the ever-present, hindering duality. While it may be admirable to seek the lofty goal of nirvana, or non-dualism, offered by the disciplined study of Zen Buddhism, most must settle for less ambitious objectives.

However, if one agrees that reality is made up of dualistic components, then the artist, after all, has little choice but to use them. What other elements are available for creation? However, a ran-

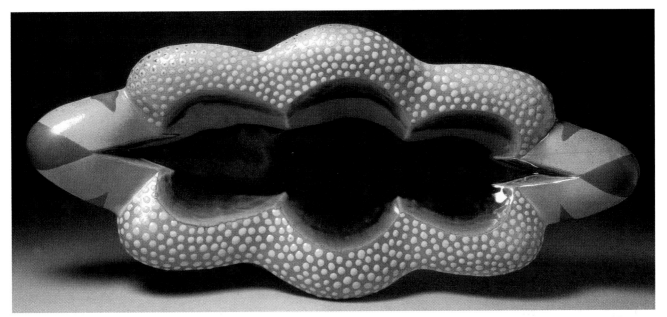

"I have chosen pottery as the subject of my art because it provides a means to explore the tension between structure and freedom, between tradition and innovation."

Mark Johnson

"Platter," white stoneware, 3" x 22" x 15", press-molded, soda fired, C.10. Photo by artist.

dom scattering of black figures against white is not necessarily successful art. It is the inspired organization, integration and, ultimately, harmony of such contrasting elements that produces such startling, transcendental effects.

But there are more complications. To say that only the extremes are important is to miss the more subtle dualities that exist. Gray, for example, is the combination of both black and white and has

attributes of each. In this sense, gray is a balance point between black and white. Leach points this out, saying: "A neutral is a line, shape or color in which opposites have already come to an equilibrium."[4] The intermediary values that lie between poles are of critical importance.

In other words, all dichotomous polarities have an infinite gradation of intermediary values. These endlessley rich dualistic elements are the framework

"In particular, I care about a sense of rhythm, evidence of process and clay, an emphasis on form, a fusion of contrasts, and tension between a restrained form and a more spirited surface."

George Roby

"Lidded Pot," stoneware, 5" x 8" x 8", wheel thrown, C. 5-6. Photo by artist.

"What I strive for in my work is a quality which, for want of a better term, I will call 'organic integrity.' This is the easy harmony of color, pattern, mass and line that one finds in a beach stone or a seed pod."

Elizabeth Lurie

"Olive Oil Server with Saucer," porcelain, 4" x 4" x 3", thrown and altered, C. 9.5. Photo by Neil Lurie.

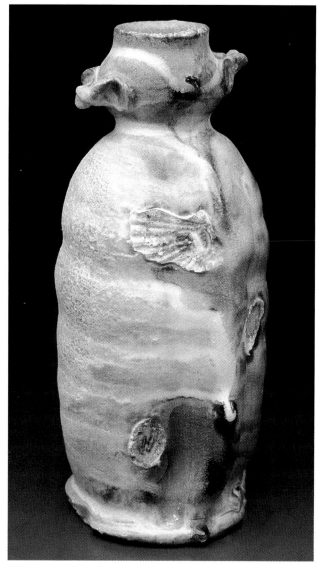

"These pots have layers of variables built into their process: side-firing, glaze application, wood-ash application, metallic salts and flux application, 15 days of wood firing with natural ash accumulation...Not to mention the variables one cannot possibly quantify and fully understand."

Dick Lehman

"Side-fired Vase: Cake-Frosting-Crystal-Wash," grolleg porcelain, 8.5" high, shino and wood-ash glaze, metallic salts, wood fired, C. 13. Photo by artist.

on which pottery (and all other art) is created.

Yanagi further states: "The Zen admonition against remaining in duality is actually a warning not to be enslaved by it, for even if one dwells in duality one may still be free provided one is the master who employs duality."[5] Since we live in an undifferentiated world where there is "dualistic strife," then there are an infinite number of dichotomous elements artists may manipulate in an attempt to reconstitute a dynamic and harmonious whole.

It may be useful to employ the analogy of music. In a musical ensemble, each different kind instrument can be considered analogous to the formal elements found in pottery (value, color, volume, etc.). And each lends its voice to produce the texture, depth and richness of the harmonious whole. Likewise, each visual element of the pot contributes a particular "voice" in the pottery expression. And each aspect of the pot must balance and harmonize with others to produce the desired expressive effect.

While this description may be meaningful, it is necessary to understand the individual's expressive intentions determine how these fundamental elements are employed. What feeling, idea or insight is to be made visible for others to experience? Why, for example, is a pot round versus square? Each form, technique or material has with it associated meaning and emotional consequences. These are the basic dialectical choices a potter must make.

For example, the selection of a specific clay implies expressive intent and capability. Each kind of clay carries with it shades of unique expressive possibilities. Why select a white clay, versus a red earthenware clay? Porcelain, for example, speaks of purity, coolness, rarity and preciousness, while red earthenware clay suggests a more common earthiness, warmth and softness.

"My work reflects a circular relationship between material, idea and process. I see it as a reflection of body, mind and spirit."
Sharon Pollock-De Luzio

"Teapot Set," porcelaineous stoneware, teapot 6.5", wheel thrown, C. 10. Photo by artist.

"Function is a limitation and a freedom. The pragmatic aspect of function establishes the parameters of form. Within these parameters is the freedom to improvise, interpret, anticipate."

Linda Sikora

"Ewer," porcelain, 9" high, thrown, wood/oil/salt fired, C. 10. Photo by Peter Lee.

seed that shapes the flower of expression. Why do certain contrasting elements appeal to individuals? In this realm there is simply unknowable potential.

For example, particular aspects of a work of art may serve a specific expressive purpose. The expressive intent of some artists may be to anger—to provoke the audience. For this kind of expression it may be useful to place sharp clay barbs on the lip of a mug. Indeed, it is a simple matter to incorporate paradoxical attributes in a visual work to produce artistic statements that are jarring, aggressive or emotionally disturbing to the viewer.

Dualistic elements may be utilized to produce either positive or negative emotional results, depending on the artist's expresive intent.

All aesthetically successful pots are complete, whole and unified. Just as there are no non-contributing visual elements in art expressions, no component can be missing or omitted. Typically, this is why a lug or handle is found at the neck of a pot. Negative space, more often than not, suggests the addition of a positive "balancing" element.

It is no mere accident that this partial area of a pot serves as a useful site for the attachment of a graspable loop. In terms of the physical balance and leverage necessary for picking up a pot, this area of the pottery form for the placement of a handle is most appropriate. The perception of "rightness" in the hand is as important as its "rightness" in a visual sense.

Herein lies another series of harmonious relationships that must come into play. The center of

The inspiration to elucidate a specific ceramic form arises from deep within each potter. This power cannot be superficially acquired and is the

"A bowl is both a bowl and Bowl. This dualism of the symbolic and functional endows pottery with its secret life of metaphors and memory and gives pottery an intense potential for resonance."

Sequoia Miller

"Cafe au Lait Bowls," iron-rich stoneware, 3" x 4.5" x 4.5", wheel thrown, C. 11. Photo by Tom Holt.

"To use the cliche that 'beauty is in the eyes of the beholder' is true only as far as those eyes have learned to see."
Robert Compton

"Tula Plate," stoneware, 11" diameter, thrown and altered, C. 10. Photo by artist.

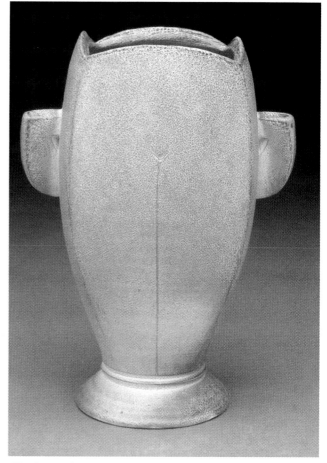

"I strive to give a sense of precision in my work, but not of a cold, mechanical nature. I prefer a more casual, fluid precision that reminds the viewer that the object was made by hand."
Peter Pinnell

"Vase," gray porcelain, 10" high, thrown and altered, soda fired, C. 8. Photo by artist.

balance and location of spots, lids, handles and lugs are instrumental in the efficient use of the pot and contribute to its beauty.

A teapot, for example, is not just an artistic expression that projects an individual's expressive insight into the world via dynamic formal harmonious balance. It also harmoniously fulfills the role of brewing tea and dispenses it in a civilized fashion. Scalded knuckles, dripping spouts, uncomfortable handles or lids toppling during a critical inclination will mar or destroy the overall aesthetic experience.

In considering pottery, the varied sensory impressions produced may startle us in their immediacy and impact. It is only after careful, earnest consideration of the visual orchestration before us that a glimmer of intellectualized understanding may occur.

In recognizing the dichotomous or dualistic attributes of a pot, we can begin to understand why it is beautiful.

However, it is first and foremost the appreciation for and love of beauty that is ministered to in this transaction. Curiously, attention directed to the particulars of pottery arises primarily from the love of beauty we discover there. This acknowledgment is no minor impetus to the inquiring mind and appreciative eye.

Inexperience in seeing, in knowing, or in doing may blind us to what, for some, may be obvious. These deficiencies can be a barrier to understanding and appreciation. The range of expression in the field of pottery is incredibly broad and varied, it is this richness and diversity that is a compelling source of continuing wonderment of art itself.

Some pots, therefore, are meant to blare while others whisper with almost imperceptible voices. These varied characteristics may be more or less agreeable to particular individuals depending upon their experiences, receptivity, culture and knowledge.

It is not surprising that the beauty of quiet pottery is only revealed in time and with patience. To see the richness, subtlety, and complexity in the best of these pots requires effort and focused attention. The gifts of these pots are only discerned by exercising patience to "see" what is before us.

This, then, is the work of the potter: to bring

the spirit to bear on a cacophony of experience which comprises the dualistic world and, in so doing, extract from it a rich harmonious expression that pleases the senses and exalts the mind. Beautiful utilitarian pottery does this.

Much more cannot be asked of it.

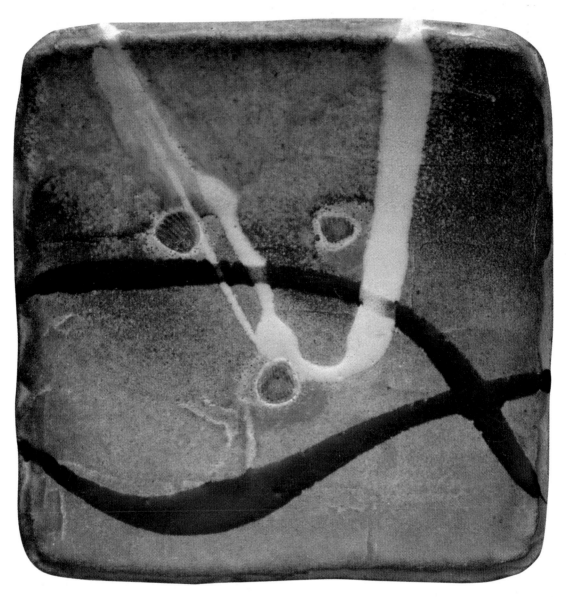

"There is in this (firing) process a sense of the nourishable accident and it is the flaw, the scar, the unintended mark that becomes interesting. The fire facilitates flawed things of beauty."

Randy Johnston

"Square Plate," stoneware, 12" x 12", wood fired, C. 10. Photo by Peter Lee.

[1] From the *The Potter's Challenge*, by Bernard Leach, copyright (c) 1975 by Bernard Leach.
Used by permission of Dutton, a division of Penguin Putnam Inc.

[2] Yanagi, Soetsu, *The Unknown Craftsman,* p. 105.

[3] Clark, Garth, *Ceramic Art: Comment and Review 1882-1977,* p. 89.

[4] Leach, Bernard, *The Potter's Challenge,* p. 39.

[5] Yanagi, Soetsu, *The Unknown Craftsman,* p. 138.

Chapter
3

Synchronicity

Repeat work is like making good bread. That is what it is, and although one is doing repeat work it is not really deadly repetition: nothing is ever quite the same: never, cannot be. That is where the pleasure lies.[1]

Bernard Leach

"I try to make up a kiln load that includes a variety of pots, including cups, bowls, plates, teapots, pitchers, jars, and vases."
Michael Simon

"Oval Plate," stoneware, 11" x 8.5",
wheel thrown, footed, rim added, wax resist,
salt fired, C. 8+. Photo by Walker Montgomery.

One of the difficulties for potters aspiring to the level of fine artist has been the question of serial or repeat expressions. Skillful, well-trained potters typically could throw hundreds of similar forms in a day and thousands in a year. Perhaps because of the repeat nature of this process, pottery has come to be considered less significant than the "one-of-a-kind" fine-art expressions.

In the past, this orientation to object making produced countless magnificent pots. The best of these works were imbued by their creators with a life force that emanated from the rhythmical pace of the potter's repetitive process. Many of these historical pots are the tangible legacy of an ancient, proven system of practice.

However, today's fine-art culture promotes one-of-a-kind expressions whose primary concerns revolve around originality and innovation. The culture disparages the work of the potter when he or she produces what appears to be an endless series of identical forms. However, for potters, this bias appears to be unwarranted.

"I consider each pot I make to exist on a continuum, to be a point on a line. A pot of mine is not a resolution per se, but a snapshot of a particular set of questions."
Sequoia Miller

"Altered Box," iron-rich stoneware, 5" x 5" x 5", thrown and altered, gas red, C. 11. Photo by Tom Holt.

Throughout history, potters satisfied the never-ending need for useful objects. It is important to note that before mechanization and modern mass production methods, everything made to satisfy the varied and sundry tasks of everyday life was made by hand. Clothes, weapons, tools of all types and domestic goods were all created manually. Thus, repeat work was often the craft person's stock and trade.

During the Renaissance, western culture began to differentiate between art and craft expressions.

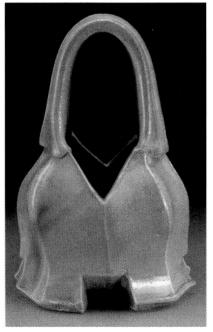

"I work in series, repeating forms with variations until they are resolved for me."
Gay Smith

"Basket," porcelain, 8" x 6", thrown, altered, soda fired, C. 10. Photo by Tom Mills.

Works produced by a fine artist were seen as unique, never to be repeated nor duplicated. Artists, working alone, created "masterpieces" in paint and stone. As a result of this focus on single, often large-scale, works, the artists acquired more prestige and status due to the seemingly unique nature of their expression.

But, by contrast, pottery meant for practical purposes was produced on a communal basis in guilds, pottery villages or as family endeavors. Division of labor in the various necessary pottery techniques was the rule, not the exception. The success of a pot was dependent upon the incorporation of many skill sets by many people who formed, decorated and fired the work. The artistry present in pottery was not born of the individual but by a community of workers, each a master of a particular subset of skills. The completed pot was touched by many hands.

"I am interested in pottery that is joyous; objects that weave into our daily lives through use and decorate our living spaces with character and elegance."
Julia Galloway

"Sauce Boat," porcelain, 6" x 6" x 6", thrown and hand built, soda fired, C. 6. Photo by Guy Nichol.

But this communal orientation helped to promote a schism between art and craft expressions since it was only rarely the case that pottery was created by a single individual working without the assistance of others.

Even though the pottery often required a group effort, individuals began to assert their individual contributions early on. For example, in the Greek classical era, individual painters of pots like Exekias have been documented. For that matter, historian

"I make utilitarian pots meant to be both aesthetically and functionally a pleasure to the hand and to the eye; pots for use rather than contemplation."

Ronald Larsen

"Teapot & Two Bowls," stoneware, 6" x 7" x 11", thrown and altered, C. 10. Photo by North-South Photography.

"Out of a kiln load of many hundreds of pots, only a few continue to ring true after several years. These are the ones to learn from since they tap a source beyond the personal and deal with universal experience."

Warren MacKenzie

"Fluted Vase," stoneware, 9" x 8.5", wheel thrown, fluted, C. 10. Photo by Peter Lee.

Helen Gardner notes, "Signed vases appear for the first time in the early seventh century B.C. and suggest that their makers had pride in their profession and that their art had at least as much prestige, say, as that of the sculptor or wall painter."[2] However, it is noteworthy that it is centuries later that pottery created by a single hand, skilled in every aspect of pottery making, is finally recognized.

The lingering effects of this fundamental difference in the nature of "artist" and "craftsman" still exist when evaluating the aesthetic worth of pottery.

The nature of pottery making and the very tools associated with its creation have contributed to a schism of understanding about the character of an artist's versus a craftsman's handiwork.

The potter's wheel was a sophisticated tool in its time, but compared to modern mass-production machines it is inefficient and rudimentary at best. The lack of relative sophistication of this tool was, in the long run, detrimental commercially to the potter. Expressively, however, the nuances of shape, color and form arose naturally from the human hand working intimately with clay at the wheel. This spinning disc afforded ample opportunity for not only replication, but also artistic expression.

While not considered mass production in a modern sense, the potter's art is certainly one of percentages. Considering the great volume of individual works produced, it is inevitable that some pieces were more successful than others. The skills of the individual, the strength of decoration, the placement in the kiln, the character of the raw

"The process of making ceramic wares demands specific time and attention, both mentally and physically. In this way, making pots has become another life cycle for me, with the accompanying ebbs and flows."

Christa Assad

"Teabowls & Saucers," white and dark stoneware, 3.5" x 6" x 6", wheel thrown, C. 10. Photo by artist.

materials, the unfathomable nuances of intuitive thought and sheer luck combined to strike one or more pots in a favorable and, sometimes, miraculous fashion.

Today, we live in an era where individual art, largely unfettered by tradition or social conformity, is the norm. Artists are trained today to break from the ranks of tradition. It appears the "new," "cutting-edge," "avant-garde," and "revolutionary" artistic expressions are the most sought-after values promoted by artists in society today.

However, this orientation toward the creation of the "new" is in many ways contradictory to the potter's art. Certainly there are an infinite number of ways to interpret the idea of a teapot. But when the idea of a teapot precludes function, then it simply becomes a visual concept—a sculpture, divorced from the pottery value system.

And as noted earlier, utilitarian values have not generally been associated with contemporary fine-art expressions. This general lack of interest in utilitarian values inherent in pottery expressions has had a significant impact on the training and education of individuals aspiring to be potters.

Which brings us to the question of the education and training of potters today.

Since a formal master/apprentice system, for the most part, no longer exists, potters receive their training in universities and colleges. This system is far removed from traditional, historical, craft-oriented practices where utility was an important consideration in the evolution of pottery form.

The values represented in the repeat work of historical folk pottery are not commonly encouraged in these institutions. Instead, content is often emphasized at the expense of skill acquisition or utility. While it is crucial to exercise rigorous discipline in order to enhance one's pottery skill level, it is not considered a particularly creative enterprise.

But the acquisition of skill provides for expressive potential that can only be imagined by those without those abilities.

Literally hundreds of pots must be made for the craftsperson to acquire the skills necessary to reach a level where intuition may speak transparently.

Historically, the division of labor in pottery production contributed to an enhanced development of the skill level of each individual. Since no single person had to master all the diverse techniques required to create the finished pot, distinct skill sets could be learned much more rapidly. While there are teams (including husbands and wives) making pottery today, this orientation is the exception and not the rule. The contemporary potter is compelled to become expert in all phases of pottery production. This requires a tremendous amount of discipline and time.

Since so few potters are trained in universities and colleges in the traditional fashion, aspiring pot-

"I prefer domestic pottery that is plain, quiet and understated. I try to make pots that will play in the background, that speak only when spoken to but carry a great deal of information to those willing to wait and listen."

Joseph Bennion

"Footed Vase," stoneware, 14.5" x 8" x 4", thrown and altered, salt glazed, C. 11. Photo by Rick Nye.

"The clay must flow with ease through your hands. If still fighting the process, this lack of technique will create a blockage that can only be overcome with a greater knowledge of your materials."

Stephen Hill

"Mugs," white stoneware, 4" x 3", thrown and altered, slip trailed, sprayed glazes, pulled handle, single fired, C. 10. Photo by Al Surratt.

ters must exercise extraordinary self discipline in order to perfect their craft. If history is any guide, it would appear the repetitive production of particular pottery form types is essential in learning to make good pots.

Some potters associated with folk traditions called these kinds of repeat pots "standard ware." Minnesota potter Warren MacKenzie emphasizes this aspect of a pottery studio, saying, "I believe it is absolutely essential to have this undercurrent of standard-ware pots, made in quantity, to support the development of, the creation of better pots. And the better pots I'm talking about are not necessarily bigger in size; they could be little cups."[3]

Historically, the potter repeated similar forms, since this was how a living wage was earned. And often times there was a direct relationship between

"We hope to solve the problem of melding function to beauty in a way that is straightforward and uncomplicated, yet not mundane."

Michael Roseberry & Bruce Winn

"Untitled," porcelain, 6" x 10.5" x 5", slab built, C. 6. Photo by artist.

price of individual pots and the number of pots needed to attain a reasonable standard of living. This tendency is reversed in the fine-art market. In that market it is much better for the artist to create relatively few, large, complex, unique works that sell for high prices.

This particular approach, however, is opposite the orientation of potters who can produce dozens of pots each day and want their customers to use pots for everyday tasks. Instead of making a few sublime creations that can never be duplicated, the utilitarian potter creates a family of related forms specifically designed for the accepted risks of day-to-day use. The creative potter is not blindly repeating shapes, but exploring specific form types in a subtle and sophisticated fashion.

The potter may also create distinctive wares for special occasions. Unique works for important circumstances, ceremonies, or for people of status in the community were, and still are, produced. For these pieces, the formal elements of the pot ascend in importance compared to the utilitarian. The orientation towards these works is nearly identical to artist's motivations. With this kind of pot, the symbolic and/or aesthetic value of the vessel is its primary justification for existence and the utilitarian implications recede to the background.

Some imagine that potters make the same thing again and again. Even though excellent potters repeat certain types of forms, an artist or craft person does not duplicate forms exactly. It would be an interesting exercise to try to discover exact duplicates of any object created by anyone in any process. (Even in the most exacting, sophisticated manufacturing operations X-ray machines are used

"Volume, shape, center of gravity, spouts, handles, feet, lids, may be all altered in subtle degrees to change the composition of a pot."
Matt Kelleher

"Four Tumblers (Blue Horizon)," stoneware, 6" high, thrown, soda fired, C. 10.
Photo by artist.

to discern irregularities that result from production variables.) Certainly it is true that potters, after years of making pots, are adept and highly skilled in a craft, but there are so many variables in the process of ceramics that it is impossible to create two objects with identical characteristics. Furthermore, this is not the aim of creative potters.

It is more the case that artists, whether potters or painters, work in a series of forms whose relationships subtly change over time. These changes are a result of the various influences that affect the temperament of the individual and their reaction to the world around them. The sentient person with

the will to create may, with luck, invest in the work a unique insight only a lack of skill in execution might betray.

The balance between the repetition required to produce forms that spring fresh from the hand and the repetition that drives the life from pots is a precarious one. Only truly creative artists resist succumbing to the deadening of the spirit. And this is the case whether one is an artist or a potter.

In a series of forms that have been thrown, decorated and fired similarly, it may turn out that only a small proportion of these objects reach a standard that makes them worthy of being called "works of

"I envision my pots residing in more formal settings in which their use may perhaps lend more towards special occasions."
Sam Chung

"Vase," porcelain, 12" x 7" x 5", hand-built and thrown, soda fired, C. 10.
Photo by artist.

"As a medium, I identify with porcelain. It is temperamental but negotiable; flaws are apparent but the beauty incomparable."
Sunyong Chung

"Platter," porcelain, 14" square, colored clay inlay, hand built, C. 7.
Photo by Paul Bardagjy.

"A cup is an intimate object to make and to use. When I return to throwing, cups come first: a rhythmical throwing process with riffs of surface notes."

Karen Thuesen Massaro

"Two Green Cups," porcelain, 3.75" x 5", thrown, underglaze, china paint, lusters, C. 9-10. Photo by Paul Schraub.

"It surprises me that after nearly twenty-five years of making pots, it is still a thrill and challenge to make a cup and pull a handle."

Linda Christianson

"Batter Bowl," stoneware, 11" x 7" x 6", thrown, wire and clay handle, wood fired, C. 10. Photo by artist.

art." This is the "search for the holy grail" by the potter. Bernard Leach emphasizes this point by saying: "A single intuitive pressure on the spinning wet clay and the whole pot comes to life; a false touch and the expression is lost. Of twenty similar pots on a board—all made to weight and measure in the same number of minutes—only one may have that life."[4] Even the fine artist, like the crafts person, must be prolific in their expressions in order to produce that "masterpiece" that stands out so definitively.

Rightly, it is only at the very end of the ceramic process that the potter may recognize the one piece that embodies all the formal elements cohering in an exceptional aesthetic fashion. This recognition can only occur when the door of the kiln is opened after the final firing. And, not surprisingly, a piece that may not have been considered as a prime candidate for success early on (or may have been tended to in almost an absent-minded fashion) may turn out to be the most remarkable of the group.

Some may suggest that few differences may appear among twenty similar tea bowls. But this apparent lack of distinction may be a result of inexperience or lack of knowledge on the part of the observer. Like any kind of connoisseurship, years of observation and study can foster a discriminatory ability that is both enlightening and sometimes frustrating because of how few artworks truly satisfy.

The repetitive ritual of producing multiple aesthetic forms based upon an idea as simple as a "bowl" lends its own voice to the potter's work.

Repeat work contributes its own cadence and insight. By being attuned to the subtle variations and minute changes that arise when working with clay, slips, glazes and the kiln day after day, the potter reaches for secrets normally hidden in that first tantalizing experience with clay.

Coupled with the expressive meaning lying dormant in the soul, one finds that the potter's repeat work can produce art work that, indeed, stands the test of time and can be imbued with the power found in any truly great work of art.

"My interest in wheel-thrown forms, altered out-of-round, grew out of the making process."

Sheila Hoffman

"Baker/Server," stoneware, 4" x 8.75" x 7", wheel thrown, shino glazed, C. 10. Photo by Bruce Miller.

[1] From the *The Potter's Challenge*, by Bernard Leach, copyright (c) 1975 by Bernard Leach. Used by permission of Dutton, a division of Penguin Putnam Inc.

[2] Gardner, Helen, *Art Through the Ages*, p. 129.

[3] Lewis, David, *Warren MacKenzie: An American Potter*, p. 182.

[4] From the *The Potter's Challenge*, by Bernard Leach, copyright (c) 1975 by Bernard Leach. Used by permission of Dutton, a division of Penguin Putnam Inc.

Intended Scale

*T*he idea of making pots without the ego of the artist is
an ideal.[1]

Warren MacKenzie

**"Simplicity is the key. There is no shock, no glitz, no glamour.
There is a subtle balance of geometry in form, a comparison of
symmetry and asymmetry in decoration, and a warm, serene
surface."**

Matt Kelleher

"Jar," stoneware, 11" high, wheel thrown, soda fired, C. 10. Photo by
artist.

In contemporary Western society, the importance of the individual is paramount and this situation is reflected in artists' expressions. However, it was the sublimation of the personality of the individual potter that was the hallmark of most historical pottery. The vast majority of pots created by people from ancient times onward did not reflect the individual so much as the broader community values held by each society at large. Pots, for the most part, were made by anonymous potters.

The socioeconomic milieu for artists has changed dramatically over the centuries. There has been a significant evolution in the role the artist, and hence the potter, now plays in today's society. Potters and pottery today reflect those changes. Art expressions that gain widespread recognition and promotion due to the uniqueness and distinctiveness reflected by a unique individual's concerns are now the norm.

In contrast, the small scale and oft times quiet demeanor of useful pots seem a liability when unfettered expressive individualism is the norm. The Japanese philosopher and aesthetician Soetsu Yanagi emphasized, "Objects that reveal ambition, objects in which lack of taste is knowingly simulated, objects where some quality such as strength or cleverness is exaggerated—these will not be universally admired for long, although they may create a momentary furor."[2]

Potters must sell their pots to make a living, and the gallery is the primary outlet for pottery of all types and kinds. To be sure, other venues, like art and craft fairs and festivals, have evolved to satisfy the demand for pottery and art of all types. And, of course, there is a broad range of galleries that sell a diverse assortment of objects.

"Collaboration has allowed us to highlight our individual strengths in a shared vision."
Karl Kuhns and Debra Parker-Kuhns

"Demi Cup & Saucer," porcelain, 2.5" x 4", wheel thrown, slips, glazes, C. 8. Photo by Jeffery Carr.

"I meld European and Asian techniques with a knowledge of glaze chemistry to define my own ceramic style."
DeBorah Goletz

"Untitled," porcelain, 4" high, wheel thrown, wood fired, C. 10. Photo by artist.

The gallery, although a relatively recent invention, can certainly be a boon to all who participate. The positive role in providing a marketing venue for artists cannot be underestimated. But simultaneously, the nature of this venue has had a subtle but important affect on potters and their work. Due to the emphasis on art objects that basically are non-utilitarian, potters, whether consciously or not, may produce work that is more amenable to this setting where utilitarian values are generally underappreciated.

On the other hand, there are a small but growing number of individual gallery operators who recognize the distinctive aesthetic properties of utilitarian pottery and actively promote this unique art form.

However, due to the dependency that potters have on this institution, the character of pottery may be tilted, consciously or not, toward a more one-of-a kind approach to form compared to the values that had driven traditional utilitarian pottery.

For example, elaborate decoration or excessive ornamentation may be incorporated to promote a sense of preciousness. While these elements alone do little to lessen the utility of the object, the labor-

"Whether ceremonial or commonplace, pottery affords a personal relationship between the user, the body and the vessel itself."
Polly Ann Martin

"Pitcher Set," stoneware, 9" x 11", wheel thrown, oxidation fired, C. 4. Photo by Frank Martin.

"The ability to use an object, of course, guarantees nothing, but if an artist understands its dynamics and struggles to create meaning inside that construct, then the possibilities for serious expression, of the kind we usually feel are reserved for painting and sculpture, seem to be limitless."

Rob Barnard

"Bottle," stoneware, 9.5" x 6", wood fired with natural ash glaze, C. 12. Photo by Hubert Gentry.

"I want my work to invite use, while also subverting contemporary 'run of the mill' preconceptions of what functional pottery is, can and should be."

Liz Quackenbush

"Pouring Vessel," terracotta, 5" x 5" x 3", hand built, majolica, gold luster, C. 04. Photo by Dick Ackley.

intensive character of the decoration increases its cost, making it less likely to be used. The use of expensive substances like gold leaf for decorative effects also implies extravagance and opulence. Not surprisingly, pottery made with precious materials will be correspondingly more dear and therefore more sparingly used.

Affectation in terms of three-dimensional elaboration also may hinder the utility of an object. A handle or spout that is disproportionate in scale may alter the physical balance of the form, making its use problematic. It may be fine that a complex, awkward-to-use ceramic "creation" sits forlornly on the shelf, but this object serves only as a ceramic curio.

"A pot in the hand is worth two on the shelf."

Mark Hewitt

"Plate," stoneware, 11" diameter, wheel thrown, wood fired, salt glazed, C.12. Photo by Jackson Smith.

In addition, the perceived value of commodities, including works of art, is often determined by rarity. This may be why it is difficult for some to perceive the value of what appears to be a never-ending series of objects leaping from the potter's wheel. This may be particularly true when an audience is not attuned to the nuances of subtle variation inherent in the repeat work of potters.

But, for that matter, excellent potters are, indeed, rare today. In contrast to the millennia prior to the industrial revolution, potters now constitute a minute percentage of the overall population. Therefore, their creations, comparatively, are scarcer than any time in human history. Since there are relatively so few utilitarian potters today, it is only natural that pottery is correspondingly more dear. This situation puts upward pressure on the

"The objective of my work is to unite traditional processes with contemporary color and form, resulting in a unique statement in clay."

Blair Meerfeld

"Flask," stoneware, 10" tall, thrown and altered, salt glazed, C. 8. Photo by artist.

"It is the private life of the individual that I address most studio efforts in the hope that the tureens, bowls, teapots and other serving pieces I make enhance the routines and rituals that frame the intimacy of our lives at home."

Gail Kendall

"Tureen," terracotta, 16" x 14", coil built, underglazes, multi fired, C. 04. Photo by Roger Bruhn.

prices of pots, thereby decreasing the possibility of their use. By default, then, may become non-utilitarian "art works" pure and simple.

Other mechanisms enhance the perceived value of objects. Obviously, large-scale works, because of their size, can command higher prices. For pottery, however, there are built-in size and scale limitations. As pottery increases in size it becomes less and less utilitarian. Eventually it may reach such a scale as to exist solely for its own sake, much like sculpture. Sculpture, of course, can never really be hampered by size limitations.

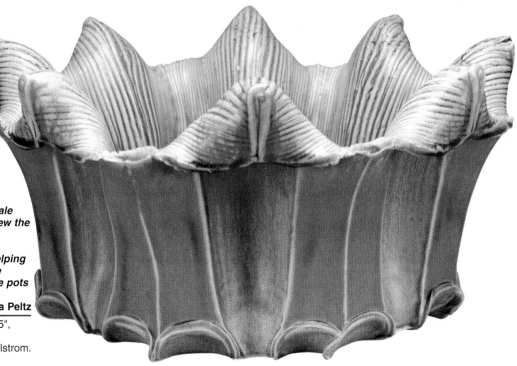

"Working on a larger scale changes the way you view the pot. The larger scale complicates the pot's association with use, helping the viewer to access the other references that the pots carry."

Aysha Peltz

"Bowl," porcelain, 8" x 16.5", wheel thrown and altered, C. 10. Photo by Todd Wahlstrom.

"I feel it is important for me to work within the traditional role of a potter, which is to say, making pots that are meant to be used. It is this aspect of craft that separates it from the other arts, such as painting or sculpture."

Willem Gebben

"Double Jar," stoneware, 6.5" x 6.75", wheel thrown, black slip, C. 9. Photo by artist.

"I am insistent about making things with my hands. A need for beautiful domestic objects and an instinctual drive to create things are tremendous dance partners for idea and desire."

Julia Galloway

"Oil & Vinegar Ewer," porcelain, 3" x 4" x 3", thrown and hand built, soda fired gold luster, C. 6. Photo by Guy Nichol.

Without a doubt, a historical element is at work in this tendency toward grandiose or "heroic" large-scale expressions. From the ancient Egyptians onward, the size and scale of art works have been associated with power and prestige. And not coincidentally, tremendous resources were necessary to create these monumental works of art. The very size of these expressions directly reflected the power of those who commissioned them. Those art expressions created for wealthy and powerful patrons left a legacy that cannot be ignored and still influences artists—even potters.

For clay artists, however, constraints on producing ceramic expressions on a large scale are substantial. Typically, ceramics expressions, while numerous, have been small in scale primarily because of significant technical limitations inherent in the ceramic process.

For example, the ceramic artist must overcome the poor strength of dry clay prior to its firing. The fragility of the work at this stage prevents the object from being moved easily without being broken. Couple this with a relatively thin cross section necessary to successfully fire the work and the result is a form of extreme fragility. The chance of destroying the work before it is ever made permanent by the fire is therefore quite good. And, of course, this is a significant part of the challenge. But a cup the size of an armchair is simply no longer a cup. It is a sculptural statement about cups and the technical expertise required for their manufacture.

Even though pottery in general is "sculptural," it is not sculpture.

Sculpture is defined today as an expression that has no utilitarian purpose (except to grace galleries, sculpture gardens and corporate lobbies). Not unexpectedly, as a result of the internalization of this definition, many contemporary potters have been coaxed into the creation of pots that are more sculptural than utilitarian. Unusual forms for pottery are not historically uncommon. However, unusable pottery forms are. Potters blend creative three-dimensional form with utilitarian values.

The prevailing orientation to contemporary art-making—that is, producing objects of rarity and preciousness—is in many respects counter-intuitive to the potter's goal of creating many small-scale objects designed for everyday use. This paradox for potters, the desire for affirmation of their creative efforts while maintaining prices that allow the object to serve useful purposes, is a challenge, to say the least.

To make pottery more accessible to more individuals, potters have undertaken different marketing strategies. The establishment of galleries by potters at their own studios and the proliferation of Web sites (see Appendix) are two methods potters have employed to reach diverse audiences with affordable pottery. Some potters like Clary Illian, for example, sell only from their own studios.

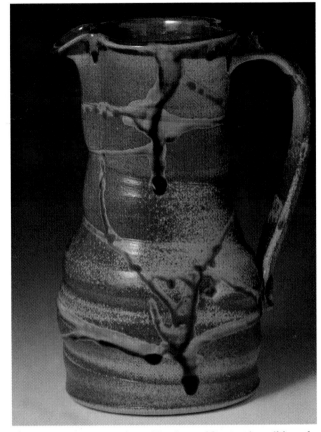

"I am particularly fascinated by the architectural qualities of clay, the permanence of stoneware, and the sweet magic that occurs when good food and good pots come together."
Dan Finnegan

"Pitcher," white stoneware, 8.5" x 6" x 4.5", wheel thrown, poured and sprayed ash glazes, C. 10. Photo by Rob Gassie.

"I am attracted to simplicity as well as complexity. My work continually reflects my reexamination of how these two poles can coexist...or not, in a given series."

John Glick

"Teapots," stoneware, 7" high, wheel thrown, extruded spouts and handles, multiple glazes, C. 10. Photo by artist.

There certainly exists a fulcrum point on the pottery/sculpture continuum whereby overemphasis or exaggeration of particular formal elements slowly, but surely, eliminates utility. When this occurs one of the most endearing aspects of this pottery form is forever lost: the ability to use the pot on a daily basis or, as in the most extreme case, to use it at all.

It is, however, on this fulcrum where the best utilitarian pottery is forged.

"What interests me least is the pot as a finished, isolated object, on stands in galleries. I intend my pots to be seen in the context of table, food, drink, hand and light."

Shirley Johnson

"Set of Porcelain Plates," porcelain, 8" x 1.5", wheel thrown, gas-reduction firing, C. 10. Photo by Peter Lane.

"I am a functional potter with my eye on sculptural concerns. Elegance of line and fullness of form are aspects I am continually seeking."

Robbie Lobell

"Cream & Sugar," white stoneware, wheel thrown and altered, black slip, C. 6-8. Photo by Jim Ushkirnis.

1 Lewis, David, *Warren MacKenzie: An American Potter*, p. 182.

2 Yanagi, Soetsu, *The Unknown Craftsman*, p. 143.

Ages Past

*T*he fine artist has a comparatively short history—far
shorter certainly than the immense history of craft.[1]
Edward Lucie-Smith

Back before recorded time an idea dawned: A ceramic vessel could keep important substances safe and secure for future use. This insight reflected the appreciation for the abstract concept of the passage of time. As a consequence of the recognition of a future possible deprivation, pottery was born. That was an epochal moment.

Ethnologist Ellen Dissanayake points out: "The abilities to visualize in a lump of rock (or clay, for that matter) a still-unformed shape and to anticipate what its use might be are cognitive abilities that involve powers of symbolization, abstraction, and conceptual thinking."[2] These powers were part and parcel of an awakened human consciousness. Thus, in the dim reaches of time an abstract art like no other emerged.

The creation of pottery requires some relatively sophisticated behavior. And, not surprisingly, the invention of pottery was only possible with the advent of a settled, agrarian society. Important technical hurdles had to be overcome to produce pottery, including the fabrication of special clay-working tools, the discovery of suitable clay, and the manipulation of fire to produce a satisfactory ceramic result.

"History has provided a diverse repertoire of vessel images which, by association, have functionality as an inescapable part."
Dwain Naragon

"Bow to the Queen," stoneware, 19.5" x 13", thrown, carved, glaze inlay, C. 9. Photo by artist.

"Early on, I developed a respect for the functionality of clay, and immersed myself in learning the intricate technology of high-fire ceramics."

Kathleen Nez

"Jeddito Black-on-Orange Bowl," stoneware, 11" diameter, 5.5" tall, thrown, hand painted, C. 10. Photo by artist.

reveals telling insights about ancient peoples. In a sense, and often inadvertently, pottery acts as a kind of time capsule, freezing in clay the diverse ideas and emotions of a society and its culture.

Many of these earliest vessels were undecorated, but their shapes often embodied robust, full, complex and useful curves. The volumes outlined by these objects clearly reflect a ready appreciation for pleasing form. It seems in this sense, at least, the three-dimensional elucidation of beauty had begun.

As centuries passed, pottery became more technically refined. From the low-temperature earthenware objects found in earliest settlements to the amazingly sophisticated ceramics exemplified by Chinese Sung Dynasty porcelain, a wide range of expressions that reflect diverse and oftentimes sophisticated orientations and techniques developed.

Plastic clay has the ability to capture significant aspects of a diverse range of paople and societies. And in this respect, the malleability of human character and culture must also be acknowledged.

The knowledge and skill necessary to produce a ceramic pot also often reflected the society's technological development. At this early age of invention, other materials such as wood, metal and textiles were exploited to make objects necessary for the routine tasks of daily life. Since one of the most salient characteristics of ceramics is precisely its indestructibility, often it is pottery alone which

Clay, since it is so easily manipulated, was utilized to satisfy many functions and needs. A multitude of shapes leapt from the potter's hand. Round, tall, thin, squat, cylindrical, flat, squared, flared,

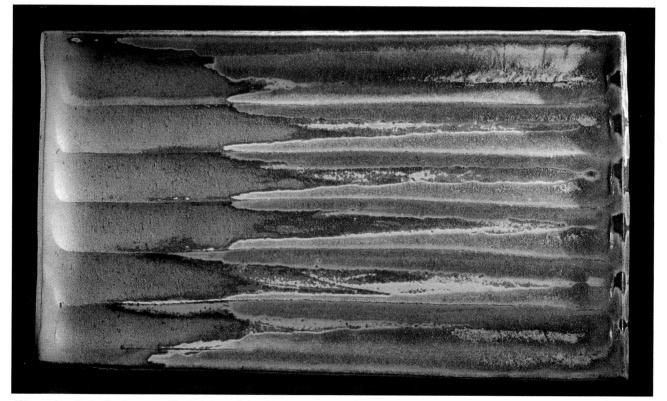

"My work reflects the forms and techniques of the Japanese art of Yakimono, the spirit of tea ceremony, and the beauty of Asian cuisine."

Steven J. Murphy

"Serving Platter," stoneware, 15" x 8", hand built and carved, poplar ash glaze, C. 9. Photo by Vito Aluia.

narrow and their combinations—all have been explored in order to satisfy particular utilitarian and aesthetic requirements.

Today it is sometimes difficult to imagine the pervasiveness of pottery during those ancient times. But by visiting contemporary cities that were built near or even atop bygone settlements, one can sense the ubiquitousness of pottery. Pottery shards can be found practically everywhere. They protrude from hillsides, flushed by rain from gashes in the earth, and can be discovered in the surf, washed ashore from the holds of storm-wrecked ships. In tidewaters at the base of Fort Jesus in Mombasa, Kenya, porcelain cobalt-painted shards can be plucked from the water: scattered remnants of a doomed merchant ship's voyage.

Even from these shards it can be seen that clay can be fashioned using a variety of relatively straightforward techniques. Forms can be derived by hand, through the use of molds, or by using the potter's wheel. Varied combinations of these basic fabrication techniques further extend the range of three-dimensional possibilities.

Throughout history the surface or "skin" of the pot was also an arena for creative exploration. Painting, scratching, burnishing, carving, texturing, paddling, stenciling, and stamping techniques were employed to produce rich and varied effects.

In the earliest cultures resins and stains from various plants were exploited to seal the porous wall of the pot as well as provide a decorative mark.

Burnishing the surface of the unfired clay was another method used to seal the pot and make it

"I choose to fire with wood because I love the forms and surfaces highlighted by the warm colors and soft yellows of the wood ash deposits."
Peg Malloy

"Pitcher," porcelain, 10.25" x 7.5" x 5", thrown, wood fired, C. 10-11. Photo by Dan Meyers.

"I am particularly interested in the way that glaze relates to form."
Rebecca Harvey

"Jelly Server," porcelain, 5" x 3" x 7", press molded and assembled, C. 6. Photo by artist.

"I make pots for daily use, so I'm concerned with tactile qualities like weight, balance and proportion, as well as visual qualities."

Sarah Jaeger

"Sauceboat," porcelain, 6" x 7" x 7", wheel thrown, C. 10. Photo by Peter Lee.

Curiously, the burnishing process produced a shiny surface that foreshadowed the development of glazes. This curious interest in a shiny, smooth surface appears early in the history of pottery.

Glass, in the form of glazes, permanently bonded to the clay by the fire, was a critical technical development that produced a permanent, hygienic, smooth, glossy surface. The Egyptians were the first to incorporate this transformative surface. In China, the Middle East, Japan, Europe and elsewhere, potters exploited and evolved expressive possibilities with their own glaze discoveries and inventions.

The discovery of glassy materials affixed to the surface of the pot infinitely expanded the range of surface enhancement possibilities. As the level of sophistication and knowledge of materials and techniques grew, so did the number and kind of colors and textures that animated the pots' surfaces.

In addition, metal oxide-bearing minerals that produced contrasting colors and values were discovered and exploited. Colored slips in the form of underglazes as well as stains and overglaze enamels were developed. These contributions lent a practically infinite palette by which artists could enliven the pot's surface.

Prior to industrialization, pottery and other art forms developed in relative isolation. The long, slow process of developing techniques, styles and

more useful. The addition of very refined slips (liquefied clay), such as terra sigillata (sealed earth), produced even smoother, harder, and more glossy surfaces. This type of ware is best exemplified in ancient black and red figure Greek pottery, but can be found in numerous other cultures.

"I try to achieve a blend of historical ideas of form and surface with my own vision."

George Parker

"Covered Jars," porcelain, 11" high, thrown, fired in anagama kiln, C. 11. Photo by artist.

"If the maker has worked well, the pot will reflect much about their attitudes towards generosity, humor, caring, wholeness, etc."

Jim Lorio

"Wood-fired Platter," stoneware, 3.5" x 19" diameter, thrown and textured, C. 11. Photo by John Bonath.

images occurred with little intervention from outside sources. The transfer of information and materials from culture to culture historically occurred very slowly. As a result, cultural expressions, including pottery, were nurtured and flowered in distinctive and original ways.

Pottery was born in guilds composed of master craftsmen and their apprentices, or inter-generational family workshops. Large, ambitious operations like those revealed in ancient China, Japan, Greece and elsewhere were common. Concerning Greek pottery, Edward Lucie-Smith notes, "We know that the production of red-figure (pottery) was pretty much factory work—a prosperous

Athenian workshop of this type might employ as many as seventy men."[3] In regard to Chinese pottery, Lucie-Smith states, "One can scarcely talk of individual expression, since it is clear that the making and decorating of fine porcelains was a complex operation in which many hands were involved, the aim being to achieve a consistent product."[4]

Entire villages were at times devoted to the task of pottery making.

Today there are relatively few production potteries like those historical operations since, economically, this orientation to pottery making cannot compete with modern ceramic manufacturing operations.

Likewise, the fanfare now associated with the individual contemporary "artist" was absent throughout much of history. Historical artisans or craft workers toiled to produce goods undisturbed by fantasies of wide fame or instant fortune. Most historical pottery was a product of hard, honest work. Laborious, repetitive, and exhausting working conditions were the historical potter's fare. But, of course, all living conditions were much more difficult due to the lack of the modern conveniences we now take for granted. Perhaps this very adversity promoted the investment in those pots the attributes we so readily respond to today.

But as the centuries passed so did the needs of those more populous and richer societies. Eventually, the slow-paced orientation to the production of pottery changed. Just as the potters' wheel displaced hand work in some cultures, mass manufacturing tolled the death knell for many potteries in recent times.

"My vocabulary is partially inspired by the loose, direct, and eccentric qualities of old Korean porcelains."

Catherine White

"Covered Bowl with Ridges," white stoneware, 4" x 7" x 7", wheel thrown, C. 9. Photo by Hubert Gentry.

"Hopefully, my pots move out of a ceramic folk tradition to express my own individual nature and spirit having energy and a life that passes from my hands to that of the user."

Malcolm Davis

"Teabowls," grolleg porcelain, 3.25" x 3" x 3", wheel thrown, shino glaze, C. 10. Photo by Ralph Gabriner.

"Butter Dish," white stoneware, 4.5" x 10" x 4", molded
and hand built, C. 6. Photo by John Knaub.

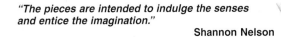

"Wood-fired Vase," porcelain, 7.5" x 5", wheel thrown, wood fired,
C. 10. Photo by David Kingsbury.

Along the way, mass-produced ceramic pottery
itself was displaced by forms made of more "modern"
materials such as glass, paper, various metals and, of
course, plastic. And people were eager to endorse
these more modern products. Economic development
today depends upon people casting aside the old and
replacing it with the new. Indeed, in this sense, pottery
making is an old-fashioned art form.

Cultural practices have changed. In modern times
the potters' imprimatur in ceramic objects, for the
majority of modern consumers, has been lost. Today
we live in a "disposable" society where things are so
cheap, both aesthetically and economically, that they
are simply thrown away after a perfunctory use.

But this convenience and efficiency has come at a
remarkable penalty. Most common manufactured
products are impersonal, cold and devoid of significant aesthetic interest. These items remind us not of
our humanness, but of the machines themselves.
Ancient pottery does not bear this defect. This is
because historical potters did not have to labor under
the yoke of machines any more complex than the potter's wheel. The cultures of ancient people and potters
were simply not that far removed from the challenges
and wonders presented by nature herself.

Pre-industrial potters had no option but to use
their hands and simple tools to create the utensils
required for everyday life. These handcrafted objects
spoke of the maker's touch and with that contact the
pottery was charged with the essence of life itself.
Unfortunately, commercial mass-produced pottery
congenitally contains qualities reflecting its method of

"I have always worked within the context of functional pottery. The implied history and intimacy of the useful pot provides both boundaries to exceed and traditions to draw on."

Kathy Erteman

"Plates," whiteware, 4-6" diameter, wheel thrown, C. 2. Photo by D. James Dee.

manufacture. What previously was warm, rich, irregular and soft, became sterile, cold, hard and predictable.

Historically, pots were produced by people who acquired the art of pottery making under circumstances far removed from the conditions in which pottery is produced today.

Throughout human history information about clay, glazes and firing processes was gleaned through the process of trial and error and handed down from generation to generation. Beautiful pots from the vast reaches of history were produced without benefit of science as we know it today, without an abundance or variety of material resources, without libraries, without universities, without schools of art, without art professors, and without computers. And yet these people created treasures.

Currently, it appears there is a renaissance in thinking about utilitarian pottery as an important and unique form of artistic expression. The quality of pottery illustrated in this book bears testimony to this re-evaluation.

"I work forms into compositions I feel have a visual and emotional impact. The process and the product become my contemporary connection to a vital ceramic tradition."

Randy Edmonson

"Vase," stoneware, 10" x 8" x 8", thrown, wood fired, natural ash glaze, C. 12. Photo by Taylor Dabney.

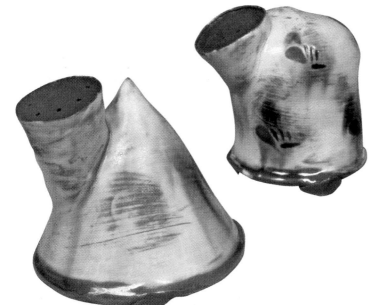
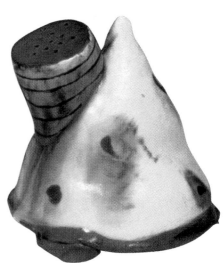

"I am concerned with the issues of how pots perform their specific functions mechanically, but also with the ritual engagement they have with the user."
Greg Pitts

"Salt Shakers," terracotta, 3.25" high, thrown and altered, sgraffito, terra sigillata, C. 04. Photo by Erma Estwick.

The best potters working today speak with the same kinds of voices that speak through wonderful ancient pots. These voices sing the praises of an appreciation of nature, hard work, sincerity, straight-forwardness, utility, honesty and beauty in personal expression.

This is obvious for all to see.

"In my work, it is my intention to create pots that enter people's everyday lives in a direct and intimate way."
Posey Bacopoulos

"Pitcher," terracotta, 7" x 7.5" x 4", thrown and altered, majolica glazed, C. 04. Photo by Kevin Noble.

[1] Lucie-Smith, Edward, *The Story of Craft,* p. 281.

[2] Dissanayake, Ellen, *What is Art For?,* p. 113.

[3] Lucie-Smith, Edward, *The Story of Craft: The Craftsman's Role in Society,* p. 43.

[4] Ibid, p. 80.

Towards Tradition

For the potter the local terms of reference, what I elsewhere call tradition, have been lost, or at any rate greatly weakened, and he finds himself alone in his search with the world to roam in, torn as it is, with the polarities of inner and outer, East and West, to choose between.[1]

Bernard Leach

"I am compelled by many streams of pottery production and tradition throughout the history of ceramics..."
Gail Kendall

"Tureen," terracotta, 13" x 14", coil built, underglazes, multi fired, C. 04. Photo by Roger Bruhn.

For all intents and purposes, the efficiencies of mass production and machine manufacture have resolved the elemental human need for basic utensils necessary for life. Therefore, the utilitarian potter's work, at least in this vein, is anachronistic.

Pottery derived from a handicraft tradition has been almost totally replaced by utensils made from newer, modern materials. If a ceramic pot is found in the modern home today it is more likely to have been produced by machine than by hand.

The mechanization and standardization of pottery began centuries ago. Ironically, the first

"I try to remain respectful of traditional form because it is important to me to be accessible to a broad audience."
Kate Shakeshaft Murray

"Feathered Jar," stoneware, 10" x 7", thrown, wax resist, C. 10-12. Photo by artist.

"I strive to create a rich dialogue between form and surface. The color and texture in my work is informed by the natural world; by moss and stone, bark and hair and skin."
Jessica Dubin

"Low Bowl," stoneware, 3.5" x 13", wheel thrown, wood fired, ash glazes, C. 10. Photo by Nicholas Whitman.

The potter's wheel dramatically raised the technical and aesthetic standards for pottery. Thinner, stronger, more sophisticated and refined shapes could be more readily made. Simultaneously, this tool enabled the individual potter to produce pots more quickly and replicate shapes more easily. The ability to create more, and better, pots in less time was, most assuredly, a welcome economic development. But this tool also advanced the expressive possibilities of pottery form.

The comportment or orientation of the person working on the wheel has always been an inescapable part of the gesture of pottery. Even though the tools are similar, the pottery-making trade in ancient times was much different than it is

mechanical innovation that extended the reach of pottery was the potter's wheel itself. This simple machine, a stone disc, rotating on a spindle, thoroughly transformed the character of pottery.

"My low momentum kick-wheel has the slow, undulating rhythm typical of the human-powered pottery wheels which were used in the making of many of the historical pots I admire."
Louise Harter

"Ruffle Edged Plate Set," local stoneware, 1" x 4" x 4", wheel thrown, salt and soda fired, C. 10. Photo by Tom Mills.

today. The potter's wheel was one of the most sophisticated machines at the disposal of the pre-industrial potter. The lack of sophisticated kilns and materials presented numerous technical and logistical challenges for pottery makers.

But, because of this, impurities, irregularities and the uneven quality of materials produced characteristics infused in the very fabric of the pots. The "naturalness" of the raw materials of ancient pottery was ever present in the ceramic process. Pottery forms were only slightly removed from nature and reflected the variability found there.

Eventually, new, more complicated machinery was incorporated into the pottery process. Technique and materials became more controlled. Even prior to the industrial revolution the anomalous was slowly eliminated from processes and material in an effort to produce more uniform, marketable results.

Eventually, mass production techniques achieved the goal of technical perfection based upon very specific design specifications. However, increased efficiencies in the fabrication of pottery

"I make work in an active search for emotion, feeling, content and form in the objects we use in daily life."
Alleghany Meadows

"Pitcher," stoneware, 11" x 10" x 6", wheel thrown, altered, salt fired, C. 9. Photo by artist.

changed its elemental character. Soetsu Yanagi has observed: "No machine can compare with a man's hands. Machinery gives speed, power, complete uniformity, and precision, but it cannot give creativity, adaptability, freedom, heterogeneity. These the machine is incapable of, hence the superiority of the hand, which no amount of rationalism can negate."[2]

In addition, the impact of the machine has also lulled us into an expectation of false perfection. Having zero defects is an important goal for industry, and similar craftsmanship or attention to detail is inherent in any great work of art. But the skillful execution of technique in art and pottery is aligned with the expressive intent of the maker.

It is for this reason that handmade pottery sometimes appears, at first glance, to hold defects. These minor irregularities occur because the materials, processes and intentions do not preclude these consequences. The clay is rough or impure, the kiln fires in an unexpected fashion, the shape is not a perfect cylinder, the glaze is thick or thin, the decoration uneven, the glaze flowed or collected, the shape bulges here or there and so on and so on. These "imperfections" can lend charm and grace to the expression and as such free it from the constraint of the infallible. However, these expressive "imperfections" cannot to be so aggressive as to be considered defects that detract from the basic integrity of the pot.

"Historical references inform my work and help connect me to the vast time line of the craft of utilitarian pottery."
Thomas Rohr

"Whiskey Bottle with Cup," porcelain, 12" x 4", thrown, wood fired, C. 12. Photo by artist.

"I think pottery can offer an accessible context for the user to experience ideas about irregularity and physicality that are missing in industrial production."
Alec Karros

"Tray with Glasses," porcelain, 16" diameter, wheel thrown with glazes, C. 6. Photo by John Woodin.

While society gained much in this industrial transformation, something essential was also lost. Bernard Leach notes: "We pretend to ourselves that we are happy when there is no irregularity, but we have killed the joy in making because we have become the slave of the machine."[3] In the modern era where people are more and more married to sophisticated technological devices, these words appear even more meaningful.

The quiet, rhythmic cadence of the whirring wheel and the slap of the clay as each pot is formed are as soothing and as stimulating as the crashing ocean surf. This rhythm of creation can also be heard in the systematic stoked roar of the wood-fired kiln.

Pottery is not only a messenger of art, but is a messenger of nature herself. The forms, materials, textures, and colors found in pottery reflect those characteristics teeming throughout nature. Many pots reflect these elements and allow us the pleasure of nature's company in the home.

"The characteristic shapes of shino ware, simple and rough, warped and distorted, make them expressions of delightful spontaneity and lively individuality. My work is inspired by such folk traditions."
Malcolm Davis

"Footed Covered Jar," grolleg porcelain, 11" x 6" x 6", thrown, shino glaze, C. 10. Photo by Ralph Gabriner.

"The dullest glaze I use has little fissures of shine running through it, like skin on custard or crust on lava. Glaze acts as a recorder of gravity, marking the liquid pull of the earth."
Rebecca Harvey

"Sugar/Creamer," porcelain, 3" x 3" x 5", press molded and assembled, C. 6. Photo by artist.

"It is my belief that domestic pottery can transform the home where it exists, for it is at 'Home' that we are most comfortable to receive information."

Polly Ann Martin

"Marmalade Set," stoneware, 3.5" x 13", wheel thrown, oxidation fired, C. 4. Photo by Frank Martin.

This concept is not a new one. Others have striven to bring nature directly into the lived life. One can see this philosophy in the architecture of Frank Lloyd Wright. Natural materials are allowed to speak in his buildings and the truthfulness of those voices articulates beauty. This continuing contact with beautiful things most assuredly has its effect on our lives. As Frank Lloyd Wright said: "Whether people are fully conscious of this or not, they actually derive countenance and sustenance from the 'atmosphere' of the things they live in or with. They are rooted in them just as a plant is in the soil in which it is planted."[4]

Unfortunately, in far too many cases people's lives today reflect an aesthetic barrenness or vacuity.

Pottery, with its literal connection with elements of nature and shaped via the inspired touch of the hand, can connect us intimately with a primordial aspect of life in a most intimate and immediate way. While industrially designed objects may have their strengths, they cannot compete with the beautiful object created under the aegis of the enlightened heart, mind and hand.

Unique historical pottery forms evolved in regions where appropriate raw materials and the imaginative human mind converged. These pots were a "natural" outgrowth of the resources discovered in a restricted geographical area where the potters lived and were products of the unique indigenous cultural values.

And throughout the production of pre-industrial pottery the individual, whether organized in a family, village, or guild context, was always at the critical nexus of this handicraft.

"In the refrigerator, on the table or in the sink, good pots act as brave contradictions to the impersonal and the shoddy."

Mark Hewitt

"Gallon Pitcher," stoneware, 14" high, wheel thrown, wood fired, salt glaze, C. 12. Photo by Jackson Smith.

"Aesthetically, I have been guided by Japanese and Chinese crafts, European design movements and simple utilitarian objects such as those produced by American Shakers."

Paul Eshelman

"Rectangular Trays and Cappuccino Cups," red stoneware, 3" x 15" x 4.5" slip cast, C. 4. Photo by Peter Lee.

The industrial revolution essentially changed the potters' circumstances both economically and socially. First of all, due to efficiencies of machine mass production, the potter was driven from the mass marketplace. Secondly, a wealthy middle and upper class evolved. Pottery was no longer produced as it had been. Instead, we see the development of an "art" pottery. The value and prestige of this new pottery was associated primarily in the quality of the painting and the appropriateness of the two-dimensional design of these expressions.

This can be readily seen in the numerous examples of the art pottery movement at the end of the nineteenth century.

In keeping with the steady rise of a "fine art" culture, the value and prestige of this new pottery was associated primarily with painting; not utility. The pots were simply blanks thrown by the "mud" man. The "artification" of pottery had begun.

As the years passed, the skills, methods, techniques and understanding of materials necessary to make pots were, for all intents and purposes,

"Every stage in the process of making these pots seems to present some new challenge for uniting historical techniques with technological innovation."

Louise Harter

"Juice Cups with Rain Pattern," stoneware, 4" x 3" x 3", thrown, wood fired, C. 10. Photo by Tom Mills.

"Many of us find comfort and interest in old, familiar things, while others seek inspiration or stimulation in the blatantly new or unconventional."

Charity Davis-Woodard

"Vessel on Six Feet," porcelain, 9" x 11" x 5.5", thrown and altered, slip, glaze, wood fired, nichrome wire, C. 10. Photo by Jeffrey Bruce.

severed from folk pottery tradition. Today, an education in pottery is gained primarily by attending colleges and universities. This is a dramatic new development. Today it is rare for a person to be intensively trained by a master potter or participate in an organized guild where specific skills or techniques are learned.

A contemporary education in pottery more likely than not, reflects a piecemeal series of ceramics courses. The cumulative intended effect of this regimine is to produce mastery in clay. While the fundamental goals are laudable, the end result is often lacking.

This system produces comparatively few quality potters because there is generally insufficient time to master the techniques necessary to produce skillful work. Instead, creativity and originality are promoted and technical execution, for the most part, is de-emphasized.

Ages ago the individual was a lesser cog in the creative wheel of practice of pottery making. In the past, even the child apprentice in the pottery knew the expressive ends to which the hands were employed. Pottery was made anonymously, and stylistic and technical limitations focused the expressive result.

For example, in ancient Greece there was never a need to invent totally "new" utilitarian forms. Standard shapes like the amphora, a narrow-necked vase, were the primary templates from which rich and subtle form variations occurred.

Although some pots were signed by individuals, the painting technique was consistent since the

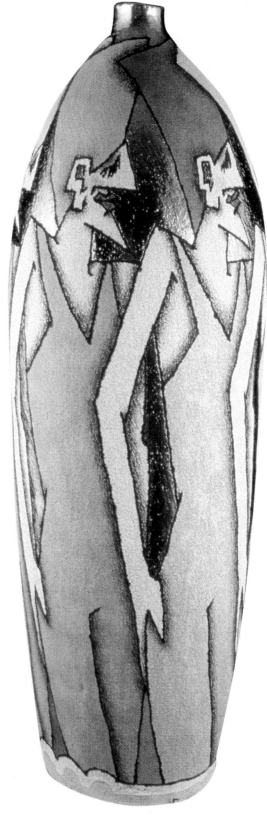

"My work is influenced by the culture I live in, the machine age, the urban environment, the media and the fad and fashion."

Rimas Vis Girda

"Plain and Simple," stoneware, 31.5" x 10" x 10", coil built, engobe, wax inlay, underglaze pencil, glaze, china paints, lusters, multi fired, C. 10, 05, 018. Photo by artist.

"I'm influenced by the whimsy of Dr. Seuss, the pattern and color in Japanese Kimono design, the textiles of West Africa and the simple expression found in ancient Greek pottery."
Meg Dickerson

"Funky Creamer," white stoneware, 5.5" x 4" x 1.5", wheel thrown, altered, C. 6. Photo by artist.

technical possibilities of the pigments and tools were quite limited in ancient Greece. This was generally true in all ancient cultures. Impressive, expressive results were based upon very low-technology solutions.

The transformation of the black-figure style to that of the red-figure style illustrates this point. With the simple reversal of the figure-ground relationship, the expressive potential to document and record important subjects was magnified. This simple but revolutionary technical insight enhanced the ability of the artist to reflect the values of the culture. It is striking that such limited technical achievement was sufficient to amplify the character, fullness and spirit of a rich and complex culture.

The most difficult part of producing good pottery today is knowing how to combine all of the disparate parts of the work into a unified, significant, expressive whole. This is the paradoxical aspect of contemporary artistic expression. Why? It is because the individual's values, not shared community values, are the essential expressive dynamo that motivates today's artists. Stylistic uniformity is a contra-indication for a contemporary artist.

Art today must be "original," "unique," "idiosyncratic." Hence, the expressive nub of the pot must be as distinct as the fingerprints of the potter who created it.

Unlike potters of the past, today's potter can choose from countless techniques, is inundated with ample materials from every part of the globe, and is influenced by art from many cultures, past and present. As Leach first stated in *The Potter's Book* over sixty years ago, "In a broad way the difference between the old potters and the new is between unconsciousness within a single culture and individual consciousness of all cultures."[5]

In the past, there was a consensus in the nature of the work that was produced, how a pot should be made, and the values pottery embodied. And much of the consensus was nestled in a close-knit community of potters who shared a life of pottery making.

Currently, there appears to be little consensus about anything, let alone in art or pottery. Perhaps the only consensual values maintained by the best potters working today are in part tacit ones: pottery should be useful and, indeed, it should be beautiful.

For our society, in this time, perhaps this is the very best we can do.

[1] From the *The Potter's Challenge*, by Bernard Leach, copyright (c) 1975 by Bernard Leach. Used by permission of Dutton, a division of Penguin Putnam Inc.

[2] Yanagi, Soetsu, *The Unknown Craftsman*, p. 107.

[3] Bernard Leach, *The Potter's Challenge*, p. 23.

[4] Wright, Frank Lloyd, *The Natural House*, p. 136.

[5] Clark, Garth, *Ceramic Art: Comment and Review*, p. 78.

Land's End

O ne must chew and eat up mingie—eat it, consume it, put it in your belly, to put it in your system and digest it is what is required in this day and age. We are to assimilate it and do something of our own with this food.[1]

Shoji Hamada

There are many people who have had a substantial impact on the development of pottery in America during the later half of the twentieth century, but none more than Bernard Leach (1887-1979), Shoji Hamada (1894-1978) and Soetsu Yanagi (1889-1961). As writer Michael Webb stated ten years ago, "The meeting of Bernard Leach and Shoji Hamada in 1919 over seventy years ago, started ripples which are still widening today and which may be considered one of the crucial events in twentieth-century ceramic history."[2]

Leach, an Englishman, and Hamada, his like-minded Japanese potter friend, discovered pottery in Japan early in the twentieth century and devoted their lives to creating pots and promoting utilitarian pottery as an art form. Their essential cohort, Japanese aesthetician Soetsu Yanagi, detailed the philosophical notions that fused beauty and utility.

These individuals built on the theoretical framework of John Ruskin (1819-1900) and William Morris (1834-1896), who reacted adamantly against a world saturated by mass-produced machine goods. It was Morris who wanted to, "Extend the word 'art' beyond those matters which are consciously works of art, to take in not only painting and sculpture, and architecture, but the shapes and colors of all household goods..."[3]

"As I lean back from my wheel to ponder a new pitcher form I've been working on, I think about Bernard Leach."

Steven Hill

"Melon Pitcher," white stoneware, 12" x 9" x 7", thrown and altered, slip trailed, sprayed glazes, pulled handle, single fired, C. 10. Photo by Al Surratt.

Bernard Leach: "Plate," Porcelain, 1.5" x 8" diameter, thrown, excised. Photo by Dan Meyers. (From the Estate of Robert Hilton Simmons, Sr.)

Certainly, by the turn of that century, America had prospered.

The atmosphere was conducive to arts of all types, including ceramics. The influence of the arts and crafts movement in England and the return to an appreciation of the "handcrafted" object helped to inspire the popular art pottery movement.

But, essentially, the style of that work focused upon the pinnacle of art practice—painting. And in keeping with the "artistic" nature of the enterprise, the pottery was primarily intended for display purposes.

Leach, whose enthusiasm for pottery began in

Shoji Hamada: "Covered Jar," 5.5" x 7" x 7", thrown, painted, slip trailed. Photo by Dan Meyers. (From the Estate of Robert Hilton Simmons, Sr.)

Japan in 1909, also was heavily influenced by Morris and Ruskin. His devotion to the values found in hand work, as well the moralistic tone he brought to pottery making, echoed Morris. Much of his thought was dominated by the idea of the "whole" man, where the head, heart and hands were joined in making beautiful and good pottery, thereby improving man himself and society.[4]

It was primarily historical folk pottery that inspired Leach's almost messianic zeal. Interestingly, Leach also acknowledged the contribution of Pablo Picasso, saying: "He, as much as any man, opened the doors of our perception to the art of primitive man by himself producing an art inspired by it, which leads to a belief that the artist-craftsman of our time must in fact be an artist and accept the responsibility of being born in an age of world synthesis."[5]

"I hope my pots would tell of hard use, occasional appreciation and that they would feel like respectable members of the venerable family tree of pottery."

Clary Illian

"Vase," stoneware, 15" high, wheel thrown, soda fired, C. 9. Photo by artist.

As a Westerner who studied Oriental pottery, Leach considered himself to be an emissary for the eventual unification of world art and culture. His, it seemed, was a divine mission.

On numerous occasions, Leach spoke of this belief. In "My Faith," the forward to a 1966 catalog of his work, he states: "As far back as 1914 I had written, 'I have seen a vision of the marriage of East and West. Far off down the halls of Time I heard a childlike voice, How long? How long? By these words I meant a creative interplay of total humanity. This was my faith which has grown stronger as the decades have passed."[6]

As a result of melding of interests that included Oriental pottery and culture, Leach's *A Potter's Book* was published in 1940. Since few ceramic resources existed at the time, it had a profound impact on American potters and potters worldwide.

This search for technical expertise in those earlier years was reflected both in the Scarab Vase produced by art potter Aelaide Alsop Robineau and the curriculum instituted by Charles Fergus Binns at Alfred University in New York. Critic and historian Garth Clark wrote: "The Scarab Vase was the symbol of the aesthetic of the age. The search for perfection and control was repeated in the work of the Binns school. For instance, Binns would throw his forms, even small vases, in three sections. He would then turn them on a lathe to the desired thinness and the exact shape he required and then reassemble them."[7]

Leach's pots sprang from a premise significantly different from art pottery and Binns' technical approach. Leach's pots were utilitarian and sprung from the continuity of creative forms derived from a repetitive organic process. The character of his pots coalesced around historical pottery traditions where a subtle and more nimble hold on process, chance and irregularity was manifested.

Bernard Leach: "Bottle," 13.5" x 6" x 6", wheel thrown. Photo by Dan Meyers. (From the Estate of Robert Hilton Simmons, Sr.)

"My pots have historical resonance within a modern rhythm."
Neil Paterson

"Jar," stoneware, 6" x 7" x 7", wheel thrown, C. 11. Photo by artist.

In describing Hamada's works, Leach noted: "Hamada is concerned about the role of the artist-craftsman today and believes in using the power of healthy traditions as a source and spring-board."[8]

The name coined by Yanagi for the kind of pottery bereft of pretense and the pridefulness of egotism was "mingei," which means "art of the people." Theirs, unlike contemporary art of the time, was to be a democratic art. In this vein, the philosophy of Leach was, and still is, revolutionary.

Furthermore, Leach understood that the traditional historic conditions for producing history's greatest pottery were slipping away. The anonymous potter would never return. Leach understood this when he said, "Thus it looks as if the future 'good pot' is likely to be made in the main by the special gifted craftsman, whom we must call an artist."[9] But the basis for good pottery was apparent: Discipline

"The pottery I make is influenced by folk traditions with an interest in a variety of thrown forms and the use of slips, wax resist, and glazing techniques."

McKenzie Smith

"Squared Teapot," stoneware, 10" x 7" x 7", thrown, wood fired, C. 10. Photo by artist.

Shoji Hamada: "Bowl," 4" x 16.5" diameter, wheel thrown. Photo by Dan Meyers. (From the Estate of Robert Hilton Simmons, Sr.)

in the craft and openness to beauty that had sprung, unheralded, from process derived from ages past.

Leach's first visit to America in 1950 was significant since it was coordinated in part by someone who would become the chief advocate of the mingei philosophy in America: Warren MacKenzie. MacKenzie and his wife, Alix, were the first Americans to apprentice with Leach at the St. Ives pottery in England (1950-52). They became steadfast friends of Leach throughout their lives.[10] A more worthy, unimpeachable and valuable American exponent of the mingei philosophy of beauty could not be found.

Significantly, MacKenzie's pilgrimage to Leach's St. Ives pottery resulted from his reading of *The Potter's Book*. Herein lies one of the more profound elements of the impact of Bernard Leach on American ceramics. For not only did Leach believe in and promote a particular kind of expression in pottery but he also was instrumental in promoting community of individuals who shared those values. This was an important event for American utilitarian pottery: an incipient tradition was forming.

Unlike university training at Land's End in St. Ives, Leach had revived a type of pottery practice cradled in the way it had traditionally developed historically.

Marion Whybrow describes the Leach pottery: "The young potters were encouraged to produce individual pots, as well as developing their skills in the necessarily repetitious standard ware which paid their wages. It was a strict workshop discipline, but once acquired, was the foundation for their own success as potters."[11]

Students flowed from this pottery at St. Ives much like the pottery itself. Much like widening orbs of ripples on water, Leach's influence has reverberated among dedicated disciples for the past five decades. The work produced by the initial wave of students like Michael Cardew, Warren MacKenzie, John Reeve, Byron Temple, was highly influential and promoted a second wave of influential potters as well.

The importance of the practice necessary to master the unique skills associated with pottery making cannot be overemphasized. English potter Michael Cardew discovered early on at St. Ives the value in being able to throw uniform pots on command, saying: "Unless you can do this you are only an improviser, not a thrower."[12] Unfortunately, a one- or two-year apprenticeship experience in a pottery like the Leach pottery is extremely rare today. According to Clary Illian, "A training experience in a specific tradition such as I had can hardly

"In my work I strive for qualities of honest, fluidity, and simplicity."
Peg Malloy

"Altered Bowl," white stoneware, 5" x 13" x 12", thrown and altered, C. 10-11. Photo by artist.

be found today. It was unique not only in its ties to utilitarianism and sound form as modeled by the past but also in the conviction imported from Zen Buddhism that the pursuit of excellence in the crafts was an activity of the highest spiritual order."[13]

Perhaps it is for this reason that Tatsuzo Shimaoka made this observation: "Between 1964 and 1982 I made a number of trips to the United States, and each time I was troubled by the progressive decline of its functional pottery. Only in

"I have wisely refrained from a public display of words, and confined myself instead to creating art—a subtle fusion of aristocratic and popular culture."
Byron Temple

"Loop Jar," stoneware, 5" x 5.5", thrown and altered, C. 10. Photo by Andy Rosenthal.

"In my work I have always tried to make the best pot I can while at the same time aspiring to emulate the Korean potters of the Yi dynasty whose casual approach to their work produced some of the most intimate and moving works that I know."
Warren MacKenzie

"Cut Sides Vase," stoneware, 14"x 7" x 7", wheel thrown, altered, C. 10. Photo by Peter Lee.

"I enjoy making pottery by hand on a foot-powered treadle wheel."

Joseph Bennion

"Salt Glazed Jug," stoneware, 12" x 7," thrown with pulled handle, salt glazed, C. 11. Photo by Rick Nye.

Minnesota, thanks to the unfaltering efforts of Warren MacKenzie and his fellow workers, did utilitarian pottery remain a living art. This was always a source of encouragement."[14]

However, the past twenty years has seen a significant third wave of potters extolling the virtues of utilitarian pottery. The continuing influence, evolution and growth in pottery today in America can be seen in the inter-relationships of potters who have a direct or indirect connection with Leach at the St. Ives Pottery at Land's End. From a seed planted years ago, a tree has grown and now bears a wide range of fruit. (See Figure 1.)

Today in specialized workshops held at various craft institutions like Penland in North Carolina, Arrowmount in Tennessee, Haystack in Maine and the Banff Centre in Canada, intensive short courses are taught by individuals who extol the distinct aesthetic values found in utilitarian pottery. People such as Clary Illian, Jeff Oestreich, Michael Simon, Randy Johnston, Mark Pharis, Linda Christianson and others offer their insights, expertise, and advice concerning utilitarian pottery. The community of potters is thus broadened and expanded.

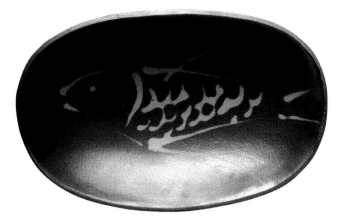

"Years of living with and studying pots of the Leach/Hamada tradition have instilled in me a tremendous love and respect for this avenue of expression in clay."

Jan McKeachie-Johnston

"Fish Platter," stoneware, 16" x 11" x 3.5", slab built, wood fired, C. 10. Photo by Peter Lee.

Other institutions, like the annual "Functional Ceramics" exhibition and its associated workshop series held from 1974 to the present, have also been instrumental in keeping alive the idea that pottery is a valuable art form. Phyllis Blair Clark, as the director of this enterprise, has played a crucial role in fostering these ideals. In addition, periodicals like *Studio Potter* and *Clay Times* have extensively promoted pottery. *Ceramics Monthly* magazine has also kept the "art/craft" discussion alive through opinion articles, discussion in the letters column and numerous articles featuring potters .

While other institutions and potters like Val Cushing, Jack Troy, Rob Barnard, and Chris Staley can be cited for the promotion and support of utilitarian pottery today, it is the philosophical and

"For me, as a maker of these objects, it is a kind of worship, which, when successful, is deeply fulfilling."

Sandy Simon

"Covered Jar," porcelain, 4" x 5" x 5", thrown with nichrome wire, C. 8. Photo by Joe Schopplein.

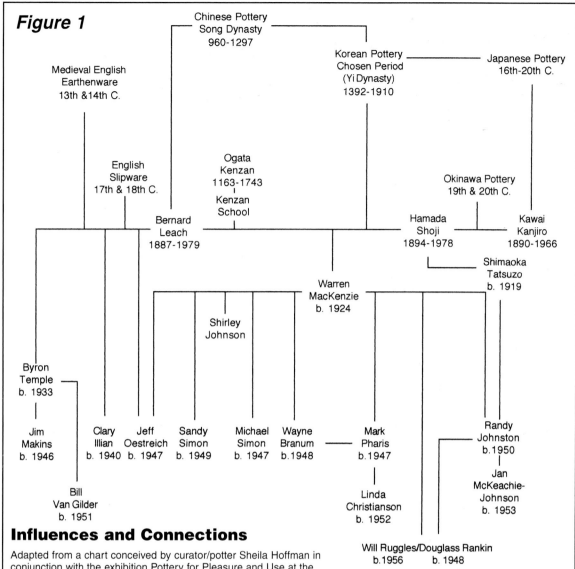

Figure 1

Chinese Pottery
Song Dynasty
960-1297

Korean Pottery
Chosen Period
(Yi Dynasty)
1392-1910

Japanese Pottery
16th-20th C.

Medieval English
Earthenware
13th &14th C.

English
Slipware
17th & 18th C.

Ogata
Kenzan
1163-1743
Kenzan
School

Okinawa Pottery
19th & 20th C.

Bernard
Leach
1887-1979

Hamada
Shoji
1894-1978

Kawai
Kanjiro
1890-1966

Shimaoka
Tatsuzo
b. 1919

Warren
MacKenzie
b. 1924

Shirley
Johnson

Byron
Temple
b. 1933

Jim
Makins
b. 1946

Clary
Illian
b. 1940

Jeff
Oestreich
b. 1947

Sandy
Simon
b. 1949

Michael
Simon
b. 1947

Wayne
Branum
b.1948

Mark
Pharis
b.1947

Randy
Johnston
b.1950

Jan
McKeachie-
Johnson
b. 1953

Bill
Van Gilder
b. 1951

Linda
Christianson
b. 1952

Influences and Connections

Adapted from a chart conceived by curator/potter Sheila Hoffman in conjunction with the exhibition Pottery for Pleasure and Use at the Ellipse Arts Center, Arlington, Virginia in 1999.

Will Ruggles/Douglass Rankin
b.1956   b. 1948

"I am a traditional potter and so I make pottery intended and scaled for use."

Sheila Hoffman

"Oval Server," stoneware, 3.75" x 7.5" x 7.75", wheel thrown, shino glazed, C. 10. Photo by Bruce Miller.

"The exciting part of this activity for me is the making. I would not like to tell anyone what they are supposed to be seeing in my work."

Wayne Branum

"Striped Covered Jar," stoneware, 4" high, thrown, wood and salt fired, over-glaze enamels, C. 9. Photo by Peter Lee.

"What I would like is for my pots to exist without question; to make pots that are so sure that it seems like nonsense to try to sum up the parts."

Michael Simon

"Hole Pot," stoneware, 8" x 6" x 3", thrown, feet and collar added, wax resist, salt fired, C. 8. Photo by Walker Montgomery.

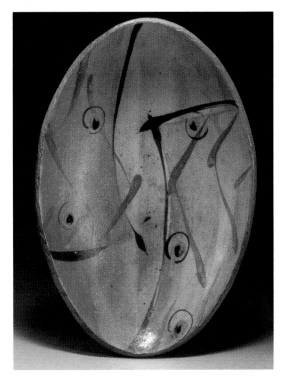

"No single aspect of the pottery process is more important to us than another. This way of potting has potential as a vehicle toward finished pots with elusive qualities of spirit, presence, and warmth."

Will Ruggles and Douglass Rankin

"Oval Dish," stoneware, 17" long, drape molded, wood fired with salt and soda, C. 9. Photo by Will Ruggles.

practical contributions of Bernard Leach, Shoji Hamada, and Soetsu Yanagi that form the bedrock on which these activities rest.

The nature and character of utilitarian pottery will never change. That is, the beauty of pottery is dependent upon the astute observation of form coupled with skillful techniques that invest in a pot not only useful service, but an element that reflects the transcendental spirit of the maker.

The pottery created in the decades since Leach passed away bears testimony to the relevance of his credo. Leach's impact on the development of American pottery is only just now flowering.

[1] Leach, Bernard, *Hamada: Potter*, p. 168.

[2] From the introduction to *Bernard Leach, Hamada & Their Circle* by Tony Birks and C. Wingfield Digby. Marston House Publishers, Yeovil, UK, 1992.

[3] Moeran, *William Morris: The Arts and Crafts Aesthetic Pipeline,* Studio Potter, Vol. 11, No. 2, p. 54.

[4] Bernard Leach, *Bernard Leach: A Potter's Work*, p. 27.

[5] From the *The Potter's Challenge*, by Bernard Leach, copyright (c) 1975 by Bernard Leach. Used by permission of Dutton, a division of Penguin Putnam Inc.

[6] Bernard Leach, *My Faith,* Catalog of Exhibition, 1966, Printed in Japan.

[7] Clark, Garth, *A Century of Ceramics in the United States,* p. 69.

[8] Leach, Bernard, *Hamada: Potter,* p. 167.

[9] Ibid, p. 167.

[10] Lewis, David, *Warren MacKenzie: An American Potter,* p. 47.

[11] Whybrow, Marion, *The Leach Legacy: St. Ives Pottery and its Influence,* p. 40.

[12] Ibid, p.14.

[13] Illian, Clary, *The Potter's Workbook,* p. 110.

[14] Lewis, David, *Warren Mackenzie: An American Potter,* p. 135.

Body Language

C lay in its responsive plasticity is so human, so living, that no one can wonder at the delights of the potter in caressing it upon the wheel. It is verily, not human but feminine. It has the coy resistance and reluctant yielding of the blushing maiden.[1]

Charles Fergus Binns

"I love the feel of clay, it's plasticity and formlessness. I am constantly amazed by clay's memory and ability to record the slightest imprint."
Gwen Heffner

"Three's a Crowd," grolleg porcelain, 18" x 7" x 10", thrown and altered, C. 9. Photo by Geoff Carr.

In the hands of a skillful potter, clay is a wonderfully yielding but exquisitely demanding consort in the dance of art. Given the astonishing receptivity of clay to the touch it is not surprising that an infinite range of expression is possible.

Pottery, because it is destined for the intimate environment of the home, has a character distinctly its own. Intimacy and the "human" qualities of pottery are hallmarks of pottery expression. This is a noteworthy aspect of the genre. Jane Adams Allen, an art critic for *The Washington Times*, has said, "What seems particularly relevant to me about ceramics is the quality of intimacy that I don't get from a painting and the sculpture. This has partly to do with touch, partly to do with the human qualities of a really fine pot that I don't find in any other art form."[2]

Merely watching a potter throw pots on the wheel is itself a mesmerizing, seductive experience. The "touch sense" associated with plastic clay is certainly appealing to many people.

Without doubt, human beings are sensuous creatures and clay speaks to this aspect of our capabilities with remarkable clarity and potency. As Ellen Dissanayake has pointed out, "Whether as ritual or entertainment the arts enjoin people to participate, join the flow, get in the groove, feel good."[3] Pots are pleasurable to make, to look at and to use.

Obviously, the tactile qualities associated with utilitarian pottery have references to the smooth, complex, and soft quality found in the texture of human skin.

"To me the pot incorporates form, surface, touch, contemplation and function, it represents the unity inherent in human experience."

Kathryn Finnerty

"Flower Vase," terracotta, 27 cm x 21 cm, thrown and altered, C. 03. Photo by Thomas Rohr.

"Music inspires an almost magical interaction between me and the clay—the best pots seem to dance right off the wheel."

Steven Hill

"Spiral Vase," white stoneware, 13" x 7", thrown and altered, slip trailed, sprayed glazes, single fired, C. 10. Photo by Al Surratt.

Potters often use the word skin while discussing the surface qualities of some pots. As potter Clary Illian has noted, "Although the throwing process makes the skin of a pot, it often looks as though the contained volume causes the skin quality. A taut, thin skin can be the factor that expresses capacity even more than shape."[4]

Moist clay accentuates that feeling of fleshiness that is eminently pleasing to both the eye and hand. The tone and elasticity of clay can be altered to produce varied expressive effects. The clay skin can move from a spongy, bogy softness to the stiffer but supple quality of leather. Different expressive effects can be achieved based upon the relative stiffness or pliability of the clay membrane.

"The surfaces I employ are intended to evoke this feeling: the sense that this is in some way a special object."

Pete Pinnell

"Drinking Bowl," gray porcelain, 5" high, thrown and altered, soda fired, C. 8. Photo by artist.

Notably, the glassy mixture fired onto the surface of the pot can provide the richest tactile analog to human skin. Some glazes having magnesium-bearing minerals known for their ability to provide a rich, satiny, buttery surface. These kinds of soft glazes, coupled with the softly rounded shape of a pottery form, certainly speak tellingly to the hand as well as the mind.

This observation also suggests a level of understated and, on occasion, overt eroticism in pottery. This is an element not often detailed but, nonetheless, is one of its most important. Indeed, perhaps the most compelling reason for the popularity in handling plastic clay lies in its soft, ductile, sensuous quality.

"My forms are classically proportioned, as the result of drawing and sculpting from the live model."

Catherine Merrill

"Tumblers," terracotta, 5" x 3", thrown, terra sigillata and gold luster, C. 04. Photo by Jacques Cressaty.

With the addition of water it becomes even more seductive due to its slipperiness. Without water for lubrication, it would be impossible to throw clay on the wheel. The analogy to reproductive activity is not easily dismissed nor ignored.

Looking more closely at the throwing process, one could say it is rife with potentially profane overtones. From the initial firm rhythmical preparation of the clay by wedging, to centering the clay by alternately squeezing and releasing clay, to opening the mass with the finger tips and finally to the

"In the past few years, my works have taken on a more figural form. Teapots and soy jars in a abstract sense seem like dancing women."

Lisa Magee Stinson

"Two Soy Jars," stoneware, 8" high, thrown and altered, C. 10. Photo by artist.

adept, gentle series of pulls of the clay to create the wall of the pot—all can be considered analogous to the play of lovers.

And, interestingly enough, the potters' wheel can be readily used to derive forms echoing the shapes of the human body itself. By starting with cylindrical shapes and then transforming them by widening or narrowing, many attributes of the human figure can be realized.

It scarcely needs mentioning, but the softly swelling and pleasing curves of the human female have been, and still are, a potent source of inspiration for a multitude of artists past and present. Certainly, there are many reasons for the fascination by men and women with the gentle orbs and softly rounded shapes of the figure. And without doubt, the abstracted arcs, cambers, undulations and other combinations of rounded forms and volumes are, in and of themselves, agreeable shapes.

The accomplished potter can replicate, either literally or symbolically via the wheel or other clay forming processes, the softly swelling shapes of the thigh melding into the hip, the arm that transforms into the gentle curve of the shoulder, the pleasant meander of the calf as it descends to the ankle.

The gradual expansion of the cylindrical form to sophisticated convex, full curves also has the practical function of increasing the usable space of the pottery shape.

By contrast, forms that are predominately concave are not nearly as volumetrically efficient and

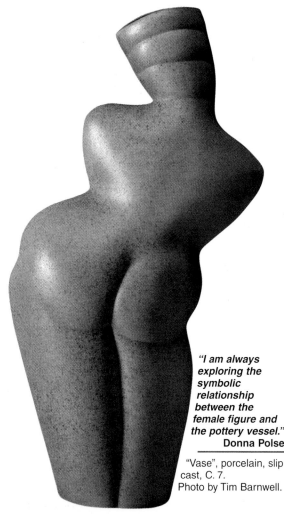

"I am always exploring the symbolic relationship between the female figure and the pottery vessel."
Donna Polseno

"Vase", porcelain, slip cast, C. 7. Photo by Tim Barnwell.

may be considered visually weak or even disagreeable. The concave curves associated with the emaciated anatomy of the malnourished are unambiguously unpleasant and disturbing compared to the rotund bodies of the well fed.

However, convex shapes are not intrinsically better than concave. The bowl, for example, contains both kinds of curves equally. In all likelihood, the good pot will be comprised of an assortment of curves, both concave and convex, with straight lines or planes for contrast.

Doubtless the spherical form represents the maximum amount of physical volume a form may contain in relation to surface area. This is useful information when the storage potential of a form is at issue. But for potters, the elementary spherical form is seldom the final determinate shape for a pot.

"Utilitarian subjects are specifically chosen—such as bottles, teapots, pitchers, plates, cups and vases—because of their familiarity and emotional resonance."
Catherine White

"Vase with Loop Pattern," white stoneware, 11" x 9.5" x 9.5", wheel thrown, C. 9. Photo by Hubert Gentry.

"I strive for an organic quality in my pots. I love to see gem-like quality, and the gourd shapes contribute to that feeling."
John Tilton

"Gourd Covered Jar," porcelain, 11" x 5" x 5", wheel thrown, C. 10-11. Photo by artist.

"I enjoy working with nesting forms and the metaphors they evoke. Two bowls that fit inside each other, or a nesting cream and sugar set can allude to human relationships, sexuality, shelter, and interdependence."

Sam Clarkson

"Nesting Bowl Set," porcelain, 19" diameter, wheel thrown and altered, C. 9. Photo by artist.

Combinations of wheel-thrown shapes including cylinders, ovoids, cones, ovals, ellipses as well as an infinite variety of forms created by hand constitute the potters' playground.

The kinds of complex curves present in pottery send important messages that may only unconsciously be understood by the viewer. As the writer Phillip Rawson has pointed out, "The fact that pots have overtones of the 'container,' 'the receptive' (in China, one of the names of the Yin), 'the generous,' of the maternal and feminine in general, must play an important part in determining the attitude of the spectator to them."[5] The impact of the incorpora-

tion of varied curves of a pot on the psyche, regardless of cultural origin, is striking.

The very descriptions of the various elements of pottery form relate directly to the human figure. The opening of the pot is referred to as the mouth, the uppermost rim at its circumference is called the lip, the narrow constriction arising from the body of the pot proper is identified as the neck, the slightly rounded curve commencing below the neck is the shoulder, the middle section of the pot, whether constricted or rotund, is called either the waist or belly, the area where the bottom of the pot meets the horizontal surface is called the foot.

As Philip Rawson declares, "And it is no accident that we, as well as other peoples, have always used anthropomorphic terms to designate these different parts of the pot, which is seen to be, in some sense, a symbolic analog of the human body."[6] Clearly, we literally embody ourselves in our pots.

The practice of pottery gives us freedom to probe these important aspects of our existence and, in fact, to celebrate them.

Considering the intimacy by which we use pottery in our daily lives, this certainly appears fitting. We embrace the bowl with our hands, we entwine our fingers around the handles of pitchers and cups, and we hold the pottery form gingerly or firmly as we bring the cup gently to our lips. Pottery, by virtue of the tactile qualities necessary for this form of expression, is an art of close, physical familiarity. It is the hand that must educate the mind in the subtlety of a pot's form and surface.

The practice of pottery making, in general, often times emphasizes feminine aspects of human

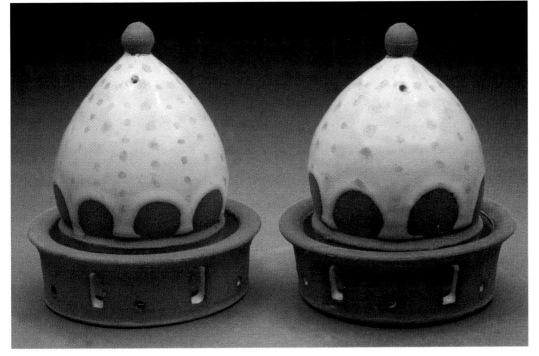

"The subtleties of stretched volume, soft curves, understated knobs, and sensual surface texture create the sensations reminiscent of touching the human form."

Steven Godfrey

"Salt & Pepper Shakers," terracotta, 5" x 3.5" x 3.5", wheel thrown, C. 04. Photo by artist.

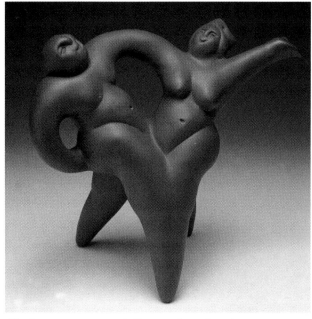

"An important aspect of all my sculptural work, teapots included, is the way forms relate and flow together. I am constantly combining and simplifying to enhance movement/rhythm/unity."

Richard Swanson

"Jitterbug Teapot," stoneware, 10.5" x 5" x 8.5", slip cast edition of 22, C. 6. Photo by artist.

existence. A pottery vessel that contains something valuable is itself an allusion to feminine capability. From this anatomy springs life itself. Pregnancy, birth and the nurturing at the breast of a fragile, fresh life are essential and meaningful elements of the human condition.

It also seems ironic that the analogy of beauty and utility, which is a mainstay of the pottery aesthetic, can be also found in the reproductive attrib-

"My pots act as both containers/dispensers of everyday materials and as metaphors for the body as both receiver and giver."

Victoria D. Christen

"Teapot," porcelain, 6" x 10" x 6", wheel thrown, soda fired, C. 10. Photo by Bill Bachhuber.

utes of female figure as well. The physical characteristics of women most associated with fertility and sexual arousal, that is, wide hips and breasts, also perform eminently practical functions at birth and provide for the infant's subsequent nourishment. Beauty and utility once again combined.

The fundamental nurturing aspect of the female in society from birth onwards is an important element of many cultures worldwide and also has a direct relationship to pottery as well. And the special role of daily sustenance is integrated to the use of pottery as well.

Pottery has within its vocabulary descriptive elements that relate to us in a direct and visceral

"The functional requirements met, the cup should also delight the eye and be a pleasure to touch."

Elizabeth Lurie

"Coffee & Bagel Set," porcelain, 14" x 6" x 6", hump molded and wheel thrown, C. 9.5. Photo by Neil Lurie.

"In music, the cord structure serves as a skeleton over which notes are laid. The familiar becomes abstracted."

Mark Pharis

"Ribbed Teapot," stoneware, 13" x 5.5" x 4", hand built, C. 10. Photo by Peter Lee.

way. Leach asks, "How do you know if the bowl is any good? By whether you will enjoy using it, not just because you enjoyed making it. Will it be nice to drink from? Does it have a smooth edge? Does it give you pleasure? Ask your body to tell you, not your mind."[7]

While the visual elements of pottery form are essential in determining relative aesthetic merit, it is the tactile aesthetic quality of utilitarian pottery that sets it apart from other art forms. In some respects this closeness to the sensuous aspects of the human experience is one of the ways that we can "legitima-

tize" these innate, sometimes suspect, erotic qualities. Just as the potential arsonist intrigued by fire may find constructive employ at the fire engine house, so might the sensuous needs and desires of an individual find refuge in the ceramic studio. Not only may people find special sanctuary in clay, but they also may find joy, satisfaction and perhaps even glory in those ceramic processes.

From the manipulation of the plastic clay at the start of the pot-making process, to the subsequent elucidation of its "figurative" form and thence to the intimacy in the actual use of pottery, there exists

"Very few things can be touched and leave one a different person. It is the paradox of who is touching whom that gives pots their greatest potential."

Chris Staley

"Cups," porcelain, 5" x 12", thrown and hand built, C. 10. Photo by artist.

"My forms allude to plants and human bodies. The volumes explore the relationships between flesh, and bone and breath."
Geoffrey Wheeler

"Bowl," porcelain, 8" x 21" x 15", thrown and altered, slab handles, multi fired, C. 6. Photo by Steve Nelson.

an unbroken sensuous strand to the pottery experience. While the cool, hard, abstract idea may be the seed that first inspires the pottery form, the sensual abounds in the life of the pot. From the pot's physical birth at the wheel to its demise as it slips from our grasp and crashes to the floor, the body remains the arbiter of this art.

[1] Donhauser, Paul, *History of American Ceramics*, p. 68.

[2] Frederick, Warren, Ed., article "The Politics of Pottery," *Ceramics Monthly*, p. 29.

[3] Dissanayake, Ellen, *Homo Aestheticus*, p. 24.

[4] Illian, *A Potter's Workbook*, p. 11.

[5] Rawson, Philip, *Ceramics*, p. 101.

[6] Ibid, p. 100.

[7] From the *The Potter's Challenge*, by Bernard Leach, copyright (c) 1975 by Bernard Leach. Used by permission of Dutton, a division of Penguin Putnam Inc.

Chapter 9

Tell Tale Form

*F*orm follows function is mere dogma until you realize the higher truth that form and function are one.[1]

Frank Lloyd Wright

"In a society that values engineered and designed products in which form follows function, my work asserts that function can follow form."
Joseph D. Van Zandt

"Covered Jar," stoneware, 12" x 12", thrown and altered, C. 9. Photo by artist.

The foremost challenge for potters is to create unique ceramic objects that unite a practical function with appropriate form and are rich with meaning and life.

When a potter faces the plastic clay, two challenges are intractably presented. Bernard Leach noted this when he said, "A potter on his wheel is doing two things at the same time: he is making hollow wares to stand upon a level surface for the common usage of the home, and he is exploring space. His endeavor is determined in one respect by

use, but in other ways by a never-ending search for perfection of form."[2]

It is the orientation towards producing forms that convey meanings or feelings that are relevant and consequential to the people who use them that motivates the potter.

In contrast to the sculptor, the potter's path is a meander whose compass headings are related to utility, and as such is not an exploration in "pure" or "absolute" form.

Instead, a more cautious embrace of form inno-

"The potter who finds life in his work finds it daily in small glimpses, and perhaps these are successes as much as anything."

John Glick

"Dinnerware Setting," stoneware, largest plate 11.5" diameter, wheel thrown altered multiple, slips, glazes, wax resist, C. 10. Photo by artist.

vation tends to be the rule. This is not to say that the exploration of unique pottery form is by any means diminished. Wayne Higby, ceramics professor at Alfred University, noted this when he said, "Limits are essential to the creative process because they trigger reaction and focus energy. The greater the limitation, the more vigorous the challenge."[3]

"The making process of the work is completed when the pot is held in the hand, dining with food or drink, connecting the maker to the user—a subtle form of communication and enough reason for me to make pots today."

Bill Van Gilder

"Creamer Can & Sugar Jar," white stoneware, 5" x 3.5", thrown and assembled, wood fired, C. 11-12. Photo by C. Kurt Holter.

And pottery is an exceptionally difficult art form precisely because of this abridgement of scope. Potters, historically, have willingly accepted this attenuated focus.

This is what Ted Randall, potter and creator of the Randall wheel, also referred to when he said, "The ontology of pottery may well differ significantly from that of the other visual arts in that what is made real is already well known in kind and thoroughly evolved...I keep looking for that degree of innovation that refurbishes, renews, connects to old Meanings, allows the fun of invention, but looks back at the past with respect, understanding and affection, opening the way for a continuous recreation of Form."[4]

A teapot, like the painter's canvas, is a known form concept containing an infinite variety of expressive possibilities. As in painting, new expressions spring into being as necessity and desire requires. While the teapot form may be the most challenging or complex, the breadth and depth of pottery-form morphology is quite extensive and compelling. Covered jars, plates, pitchers, vases, bottles, etc. all have infinite form possibilities.

The morphology of shapes available to the potter and their expressive impact in a particular form can be subtly creative and demanding. Philip Rawson indicates this when he says, "The addition of a long neck, a special lip, a lid, handles, or a spout to either the small rounded or cylindrical jar

"Form comes first, and has always been the most essential element in my work. My sources are usually traditional and utilitarian, dealing with containment."
                                                    Brad Schwieger

"Cut Vase," stoneware, 17" x 11" x 4", thrown and altered, soda fired, C. 10. Photo by artist.

can further radically modify the expression of any of these developed shapes."[5]

The potter's challenge is to create innovative, unique and significant expressive form while retaining the rather conservative yet essential values of utility that have persisted historically.

What then, is a "good" pot? While it may not possible to outline specific attributes for every case, it is true that good pottery will reflect the contrasting characteristics of both reason and imagination. In this vein, Wayne Higby has noted, "Harmonizing the dual forces of imagination and logic lies at the center of all artistic labor. The utilitarian pot is one of humanity's most enduring examples of how this duality is reconciled to achieve objects of intelligence and beauty."[6]

While logic and imagination must be present in the creation of pottery (and in its comprehension and criticism) it is the specific formal attributes of color, volume, texture, etc. of the pot that give rise to our strong attachment to pottery. Potters arrange these formal elements of the pot in most compelling ways.

"I am still thrilled at the anticipation of seeing a dining table set with special plates and serving pieces made to play a part in the gathering together of family and friends."
                                                    Richard Hensley

"Teapot," porcelain, 5" x 11" x 4", thrown and altered, hand painted, C. 10. Photo by Tim Barnwell.

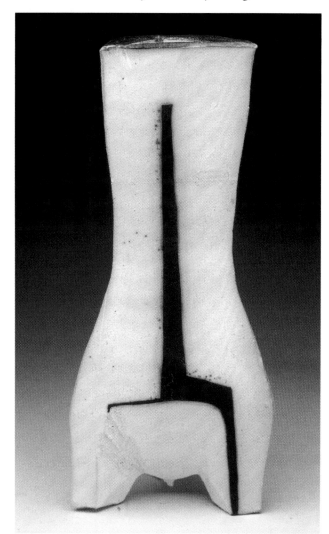

"The choices I have made in attempts to attain a more specific expression include the color, texture, and density of the clay, the shape, proportion and scale of the pot from the specific treatment of the surface and the temperature and atmosphere of the fire."

Michael Simon

"Three Leg Vase," stoneware, 10" x 4.5", thrown, faceted, wax resist, salt fired, C. 8+. Photo by Walker Montgomery.

If the previous discussion of the dualistic nature of human experience has any credence, then it may come to our aid at this time. Whether the artist realizes it or not, harnessed within the successful pot are often clusters of opposing particularities that promote dynamic, intense and long-lasting effects in the user/viewer.

For example, the round full form of a covered jar may have surface decoration composed of sharp, delicate lines. Alternately, it may be found that strong geometric, angular pottery shape may have a soft, blushing glaze languidly coating its surface. Another piece may be more aggressive three-dimensionally, but the surface may be left unglazed and therefore muted. Perhaps the major contrasts will

involve form elements alone, as when the narrow neck of a bottle contrasts with the spherical body of the form.

Sometimes it is difficult to discern the oppositional characteristics of a pot. They may be subtle or slight. The contrasting elements may be juxtapositions of overall form against individual shape, horizontals against verticals, color against form, warm color against cool, complex line against simplified form, rough texture against smooth, or a complex combination of numerous antipodal qualities acting together. These forces, seemingly in opposition, can provide aesthetic convergence when integrated in an appropriate proportional manner.

"Recently, my attention has turned to the more sculptural aspects of pots and the development of color in the surface decoration."
Jan McKeachie-Johnston

"Vase," stoneware, 11" x 5" x 4.5", thrown and altered, wood fired, C.10. Photo by Peter Lee.

"My primary concern in making pottery is clarity of form and surface, which is why I continue to be drawn to the everyday early pot in history that bears uncommon beauty and a sense of energy."

Sheila Hoffman

"Cake/Cheese Server," stoneware, 1" x 10.75", wheel thrown, shino glazed, C. 10. Photo by Bruce Miller.

Three-dimensional forms and volumes will have particular emotional resonance. The various kinds of volumes at the disposal of the potter, whether open or closed, wide or narrow, stout or thin, speak volumes about the mood of a particular pot. Low, wide forms often have a sense of stability and gravity that is directly related to the inescapable force

that so dramatically effects the throwing of the soft clay on the wheel.

Opposite of this form, in volume as well as feeling, is the slim, attenuated pot that derives its emotional impact by balancing lightly on a narrow foot and springing heavenward with an open, up-turned mouth.

Pots speak to our emotions in subtle and distinct ways. And as noted, the reference to the human body is an either an implied or literal aspect in many of these forms. And these elements may have emotionally affective implications.

The emotional feeling instilled in a pot can run from a soothing, soft, quietness to a tense, animated, chaotic feeling and anything in between. These are choices the potter makes, either consciously or intuitively, and are influenced by each artist's personality, education, and background.

In addition, the character of a pot will also be dramatically influenced by the techniques utilized to bring it into being. The potter's wheel will produce a certain kind of form, while a hand-built object will exhibit its own unique characteristics.

The potter's wheel, with its locus of spinning clay, will produce volumes that are related directly

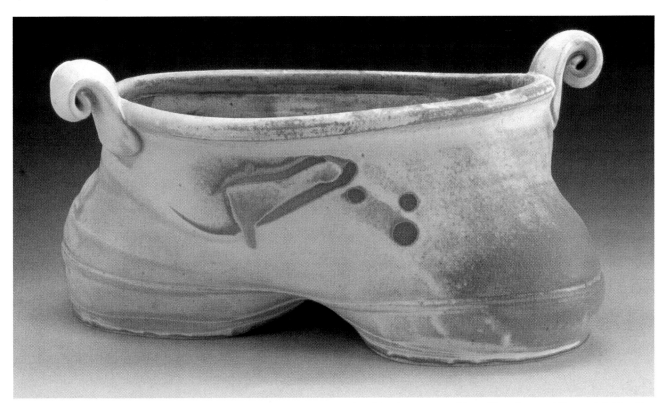

"I love how elusive good form can be...I appreciate the freedom provided by the opportunities of function, and I'm grateful for the focus that comes with the boundaries."

Nick Joerling

"Serving Dish," stoneware, 6" x 6" x 12", thrown and altered, C.10. Photo by Tom Mills.

"My quiet personality seems to flow into my work—the pots tend to whisper, rather than shout."
Connie Christensen

"Sake Bottle," porcelain, 6" x 8.5", thrown, wood fired, C. 10. Photo by John Bonath.

to the cylinder. Practically all the utilitarian forms produced via the wheel—be they bowls, bottles, covered jars, mugs, teapots, vases etc.—spring from this basic form premise.

In recent decades there has been, however, a significant trend towards asymmetrical form by combining various hand-building techniques with the wheel. Today, we see non-cylindrical shapes as well as flattened pottery forms that originally had their impetus from the wheel but are no longer cylindrical in character. This orientation to pottery has opened up an entirely new panoply of forms that had not, historically, been previously explored.

Potters who use hand-building techniques produce works with characteristics distinctly different than those produced on the wheel. More angular forms that are more architectural in feeling can arise. In working with softer slabs of clay, a potter can create more organic forms that speak to a hybrid of soft/hard volumes and shapes.

Obviously, the particular characteristics of pots must correspond to the uses for which the form is intended. A pitcher, among other things, will need a handle and attenuated lip. These appendages then become arenas for creative form exploration and expression. For every type of service for which a pot is created, complex design problems as well as meaningful expressive opportunities arise. And these design elements must be integrated harmo-

"We share a love of functional pottery and work to make the best pots we can."
Karl Kuhns and Debra Parker-Kuhns

"Coffee Set," porcelain, 9" x 8" x 6", thrown, assembled colored slips, C. 8. Photo by Jeffrey Carr.

"Soft, lobed forms and botanical references in the work arise from an interest in nature. Eighteenth and nineteenth century European presentation porcelain, sliver work and costume are also an inspiration."

Shannon Nelson

"Creamer and Sugar," white stoneware, 5" x 6" x 3.25", thrown, altered, molded, hand built, C. 6. Photo by John Knaub.

niously into the entire form.

Indeed, pots must serve their intended practical purpose well in order to be considered successful. For pottery, aesthetic success is only partial success.

The potter's expressions, in each and every case, serve explicit everyday requirements in many different ways and can take numerous forms. Cups, plates, bowls, pitchers, bottles, covered jars, mugs, tumblers, trays, pitchers, ewers, teapots, jugs, vases, tea bowls, decanters, sauce boats are just a few examples. A myriad of other specialized forms like saki bottles and cups, for example, have been conceived for more specific purposes or arise out of distinct cultural traditions, practices and needs.

It is the initial idea of a shape applied to a particular use that first motivates the exploration of

"I use the potter's wheel as my primary means of forming parts. The work is then personalized through the assembling, altering and decoration of the forms."

Neil Paterson

"Covered Box," stoneware, 5" x 8" x 6", thrown and altered, wood fired, C. 12. Photo by artist.

"The basis of what I do is about form. Without form, nothing that happens later will matter, no glaze or firing process will save a weak form."

Larry Davidson

"Oval Form," stoneware, 8" x 5" x 4", thrown and altered, ash glaze, wood fired, C. 9. Photo by Margot Geist.

"I intend my pots to function at several levels. First I strive to make everyday objects for the home and I also intend my pots to embody my own experiences, attitudes and values."
Victoria D. Christen

"Cookie Pail," porcelain, 10" x 6" x 6", wheel thrown, soda fired with wire and rubber ball, C. 10. Photo by Bill Bacchuber.

"I've been a potter for thirty years. The more pots I make, the harder it is to say anything about them."
Clary Illian

"Coffee Pot", stoneware, 11" high, wheel thrown, soda fired, C. 9. Photo by artist.

plastic three-dimensional form. This is the way in which the rational and the intuitive join together to give impetus to artistic creation.

The number of possible forms available to the potter to explore may at first appear to be limited. This, however, is an illusion. For the energetic, expressive, skilled artist there are an infinite variety of pleasurable pottery possibilities.

The potter's beautiful forms actually function. Our only duty, as lovers of this kind of artistic expression, is to take hold of them and enjoy.

[1] Wright, Frank Lloyd, *The Natural House*, p. 20.

[2] From the *The Potter's Challenge*, by Bernard Leach, copyright (c) 1975 by Bernard Leach. Used by permission of Dutton, a division of Penguin Putnam Inc.

[3] Higby, Wayne, *Ceramics Monthly*, 'Useful Pottery', p. 51.

[4] Randall, Ted, *Ceramics Monthly*, 'Being and Meaning', p. 28.

[5] Rawson, Philip, *Ceramics*, p. 97.

[6] Higby, Wayne, *Ceramics Monthly*, 'Useful Pottery', p. 54.

Chapter 10

Hand To Hand

*F*irst we must overcome the inhibitions of our Western civilization that cause us to feel knowledge by touch is immature, primitive, and even illegal. Among many other peoples the hand is a live instrument of experience, used in daily life to hold, lift, grip, and explore. As a tool for living, it becomes a tool for knowing.[1]

Warren MacKenzie

"The weight of a cup in your hand, the feel of its surface on your skin, and its touch on your lips are all essential elements in the aesthetic experience of utilitarian pottery."
Steven Roberts

"Bourbon Cups," porcelain, 3.5" high, thrown and altered, soda fired, C. 11. Photo by artist.

As a result of their predisposition towards use, pots must, without doubt, exhibit unified formal and tactile attributes that will enrich the user's experience. A utilitarian pot must be able to perform all of its tasks with certain grace and efficiency.

Thus, one finds a certain "fitness" to a pot that is not unlike the character of an animal found in the wild. In nature, where the principle of "survival of the fittest" applies, it is unusual to find a flawed or unhealthy animal.

So it is with pots. Pottery too fragile, too complex, technically deficient or disproportionately featured is likely to succumb to everyday hardships.

Generally, a pot meant for use requires that an element of robustness and strength be built into it. However, there are innumerable types and degrees of use. A pot can be used day after day, or infrequently. The extent of intended usage often outlines the expressive parameters a pot often reflects. And the decision about the degree of usefulness of a pot is often made well before the potter's hand touches the clay.

The more "sculptural" pots are less likely to be used on a regular basis simply because their forms are less amenable to frequent handling. On the other hand, a more sculpturally conservative pot, while more durable, risks being visually bland. For the potter, recognizing the balance between these

"Admirable pots, old and new, possess many like qualities; a subtleness of form in relation to a specific function; an impeccable match of surface to form; a true and correct 'heft' or weight when held in the hand and a sureness of craftsmanship."

Bill Van Gilder

"Tea Pot with Top Handle," white stoneware, 11" x 7", thrown and assembled, wood fired, C. 11-12. Photo by C.Kurt Holter.

"I make pots with intention that they will be used. Beginning with a vessel in mind, an idea is formed for how it will function in relation to human touch."

John Skelton

"Stacked Bird Box," stoneware, thrown and altered, C. 10. Photo by artist.

"Function is a condition of the pots I make. They are fashioned with an honest concern for interior volume, the kinetics of handles, lids, spouts and with anticipation of stance and manner."

Linda Sikora

"Milk Pitcher and Sugar Pot," porcelain, 8" high, wheel thrown, salt glazed, C. 10. Photo by Peter Lee.

dichotomous aspects is necessary—and inherently demanding.

While the idea of practical use acts to moderate the design of pottery, that doesn't mean that pots necessarily become "streamlined" or that function must dictate form. The Bauhaus mentality of modern design, whereby form was strictly derived from the object's serviceable features, has, in many respects, been abandoned. Stated more optimistically, this orientation can be seen simply as another option for the creative artist.

For example, the diminutive lug handles of a ceramic jar may be made too small to serve a useful purpose, but they may loom large in the aesthetic success of the pot. Formal elements of a pot may not strictly serve utilitarian purposes, but instead lend themselves to the harmony, balance or unity in the aggregate of the overall expression.

The fact that useful pottery is meant to be picked up places certain limitations on scale and weight. Heavy and large ceramic objects are definitely unsuitable for manual activities. Potters who emulate the expressive freedom of painters and sculptors often produce works that, just by virtue of

"I have always been drawn to the functional object. I seek the age-old marriage of elegant function and visually interesting form."
Paul Eshelman

"Individual Teapots," red stoneware, 4.5" x 7.5" x 5", slip cast, C. 4. Photo by Peter Lee.

their weight, can serve only aesthetic purposes.

But as critic and writer Jane Adams Allen has pointed out, "One of the problems is that many ceramists are so busy trying to compete with painters and sculptors on sheer visual impact, that they forget these tactile qualities, this intimacy and

sensibility that is uniquely part of pottery. That seems to me a terrible sacrifice for a rather dubious gain."[2]

This tactile familiarity associated with pottery is an essential aspect of its attraction. The touch response to the pot is based upon the relative thick-

"My current work is thrown and altered either by faceting, stretching, or cutting and rejoining."
Jeff Oestreich

"Vase," stoneware, 9" x 6" x 5", thrown and altered, soda fired, C. 10. Photo by artist.

"In much of my work the traditions of sculpture and function come together in a way that transcends ordinary ornamentation."
Richard Swanson

"Proud Catch," teapot, stoneware, 8" x 5.5" x 9", slip cast edition of 22, C. 6. Photo by artist.

"It is a joy to watch someone examine my pots, turning a mug or a bowl around in their hands. Clues to the making are slowly revealed by a fingerprint, a seam, an indentation."
Sara L. Patterson

"Cup & Saucer," stoneware,
4" x 5" x 5", wheel thrown, soda fired,
C. 10. Photo by D. James Dee.

ness of the clay wall in relation to the overall surface area and thus the volume of the pot. If the clay wall is thick and the pot is small in scale then the pot will be inordinately heavy and uncomfortable in the hand. This is particularly true for items like cups, mugs, pitchers, bowls, etc.

This particular defect naturally manifests itself quite frequently in the work of beginning potters. It is one of the reasons that when first learning the craft, individuals are encouraged, or preferably, required, to make as many pots as possible. Consequently, with the acquisition of throwing skill,

a thick pottery wall can be a choice, not an inadvertent result. As in other areas of the ceramic process, the lifelong acquisition of a broad range of skills simply increases the expressive repertoire of the potter.

For individuals familiar with handmade pottery, just lifting the pot can provide cogent information about the skill of the potter. Typically an inexperienced potter will throw a form leaving too much clay near the foot. While not apparent to the eye, this extra weight is readily discerned by the hands. As a result, the form instantly becomes a disap-

"Some forms are simple, others complex but they are all part of the monthly cycle of work made in the studio. Day in, day out, cycle by cycle, year by year, the continuous involvement with this work brings about a slow natural development of form."
Ellen Shankin

"Tureen," stoneware,
11" x 12", wheel thrown,
C. 9. Photo by Tim Barnwell.

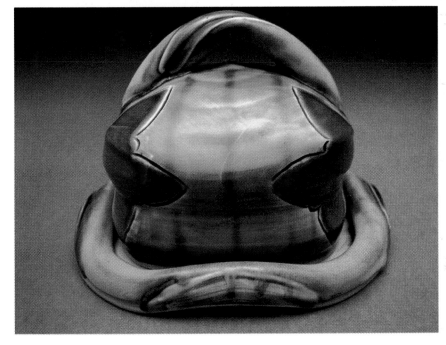

"I want people to use my pots in their kitchens and on their tables, to hold them and feel their weight and substance. In short, to take as much pleasure in their use as I feel when making them."

Diane Kenney

"Covered Jar," porcelain, 10" x 7", thrown, wood fired, C. 10-11. Photo by artist.

pointment. Most people in picking up a pot can readily discern precisely where excess clay may reside—even with eyes closed! The tactile qualities expressed in relation to the size of the form give argument to the rightness of a pot.

Philip Rawson reveals that this sense was highly developed in Chinese culture when he writes, "For example, the Sung connoisseur might like his pots to 'weigh'—and to feel—some like heavy jade (celadons, Chun) and others like lighter silver ware (Jing). Later the Ming might still prefer a pot to feel 'solid.' But by the eighteenth century, there had begun that cult for utterly refined porcelains weighing very little for their size, which culminated in the famille rose, eggshell wares of the Yung-cheng and the Chien-lung periods. Here the contrast between weight and size—achieved, of course, by turning and shaving—is extreme, and to the hand most pleasurable."[3]

Pots can be heavy or light, depending upon the expressive and utilitarian intentions. Plates, casseroles and baking dishes often exhibit heavier wall cross sections to strengthen them against damage. Unless there are specific reasons for additional weight in a particular form, it should be eliminated early in the ceramic process.

But this is not to say that the wall of the pot or its skin needs to be a consistent thickness from the

"My intent is to inspire contemplation and to celebrate use through a collaborative dialogue between the user and my pots."

Joan Bruneau

"Butter Dish," earthenware, 5" high, thrown and constructed, white slip, polychromed glazes and terra sigillata, C. 04. Photo by artist.

"When I cut into one of my works the piece is thick where it needs to be for support and thin where there's no stress. Just like our bones."
I.B. Remsen

"Place Setting", iron mountain agate, dinner plate 11.5" diameter, wheel thrown, C. 10. Photo by Bob Foran.

foot to the lip. On the contrary, many of the most expressive characteristics of pottery form demonstrate variations in thickness at critical places in the form. Deviations in wall thickness can also serve to strengthen the pot itself.

Clary Illian explains, "...we might say that the stacked shapes within the walls are the bones of a pot, and, like bones, they modulated from thick to thin and complex joints that provide the strength to hold up the body and allow for movement or, in pottery terms, changes of direction."[4]

As the thickness of the clay wall can vary through the form, the thickness of the clay at the termini of pottery is also important. For example,

"I make pots for use—bowls for soup or cereal, cups for tea or wine—all meant as much for the hand as for the eye."
Shirley Johnson

"Set of Square Stoneware Bowls," stoneware, 6" x 3.5", wheel thrown, gas reduction firing, C. 10. Photo by Peter Lane.

"Using few available materials and basic ceramic techniques, I make my functional pots in restraint."
Ashley Kim

"Casserole," stoneware,
6" x 7.5" x 7.5", wheel thrown, salt fired,
C. 10. Photo by the artist.

the emotional response to the sharpened lip of a mug is quite different than to the lip that has a fat, bulbous quality. While the thin, knife-edge lip of a porcelain bowl speaks to the delicacy of the object, it lessens its utility by being more easily damaged.

The proportional elements of pottery include weight and size and the particular relationships among all of the other shapes of the form. Depending upon the artist's expressive intent and utilitarian motives, some aspects of pottery—a spout for instance—can articulate dynamic movement. In contrast, the looping handle on the opposite side of the form will lend a visual counter-balance to that longitudinal or diagonal visual thrust. Platters, covered jars and canisters may have appendages that speak to both the hand and eye as well as unify or bring contrast to the form.

There can be no single standard in regard to the proportional rightness of any particular element in the interplay of the attributes of pottery. But the measure of a pot's success surely lies in the harmonious balance and unity of all aspects of the pot as it befits the expressive intent of the artist. And this is determined by the particular emotion, thought, idea or feeling that the artist wishes to communicate. The potter's

"We hope for pots that enhance the user's life in a quiet and pleasurable way over many years—pots whose stories never fully unfold."
Will Ruggles and Douglass Rankin

"Pitcher," stoneware, 12" high, thrown, wood fired with salt and soda, C. 9. Photo by Will Ruggles.

"My personal style continues to evolve because of the versatile nature of clay."
Lynn Smiser-Bowers

"Tiny Teapot with Spotted Spout," porcelain, 6" x 7" x 5", wheel thrown, pulled handle, reduction glazes, C. 10. Photo by E.G. Schempf.

manipulation of weight and proportion are essential means by which these notions are intimately communicated. Pottery, quite comfortably, resides between the efficiencies of tools necessary for work and the splendors desired for artistic expression.

Each gesture found in the pot is important since it is the culmination of these gestures that cre-ates the ultimate aesthetic effect. Whether the gesture is large or small, chaotic or ordered, austere or rich, heavy or light, the choices each potter makes about the weight and proportion of utilitarian pots are nestled in the dual needs of both expressive and utilitarian purpose.

[1] Lewis, David, *Warren MacKenzie: an American Potter*, p. 184.

[2] Frederick, Warren, *Ceramics Monthly*, "The Politics of Pottery," p. 29.

[3] Rawson, Phillip, *Ceramics*, p. 88.

[4] Illian, Clary, *The Potter's Workbook*, p. 26.

Choice Surfaces

From the time men and women first made pottery, they balanced qualities of surface, form, and color to make vessels and objects expressive of human feeling. The vessel requires its maker to pay equal attention to surface and form and in the best ceramic art the two qualities complement each other in a reciprocal, yin-yang relationship.[1]

Michael McTwigan

"I am interested in the relationship between ornamentation and approachability: the effect of decoration and form on function and vice versa."

Kristen Kieffer

"Basket," porcelain, 11" x 8" x 9", hand built, C. 10. Photo by artist.

While three-dimensional form arises almost magically from the potter's hand, the dynamic range of surface possibilities offer further enchantments. The selection of subject matter for pottery whether it be abstract, geometric, organic, representative, symbolic, surrealistic, or process oriented is clearly an individual's choice today.

All of the past practices and imagery of historical potters are available for inspiration and incorporation in a potter's work as well. An incredibly broad range of ceramic materials and techniques, whether found in books, workshop setting or school, is accessible for the potter to explore.

The breadth of pottery mark-making techniques available to the potter has never been greater. In addition, a vast inventory of ceramic materials produced by various commercial interests is also readily available.

For example, colored clay slips carved or excised from the clay in combination with unique imagery can

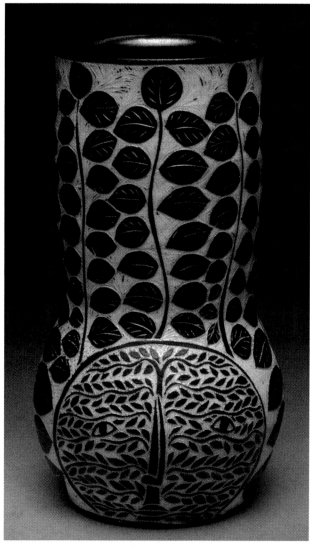

"The carved and drawn surfaces of my pots function decoratively but attempt to be relevant to contemporary life."
Matthew Metz

"Vase," porcelain, 14" high, thrown, wood/oil/salt fired, C. 10. Photo by Peter Lee.

"I was electrified by the prehistoric and early Chinese urns I studied as an undergraduate. The thrilling dynamic of fullness of form enriched by culturally significant decoration become my own measure."
Elenora Eden

"Tripoidal Lidded Cauldron," whiteware, 9" x 10" x 10", thrown, underglazes, carving, resists, pencils, C. 04. Photo by George Leisey.

"My pots seem right—approach beauty—when they have qualities of sensuality, compassion, humor and risk."
Nick Joerling

"Vase," stoneware, 12" x 4.5" x 5", thrown and altered, C. 10. Photo by Tom Mills.

produce rich and wonderful effects.

Numerous resist, decal and transfer techniques can produce varied textures, patterns or images. Inlaid and laminated clays may be used expressively and spray guns, airbrushes or sand blasters may be deployed for still other effects. On the other hand, subtle mat glazes can soften and simplify the skin of a pottery form.

In addition, the kiln itself can be used to create scorch marks, patterns and textures on the surface of the clay.

Content in pottery may be expressed with classical techniques of subtly drawn images that seem to float on surface of the clay.

But the relationship between pottery form and surface decoration is one of the most complex and

"I am drawn to wood and soda firing because of the beauty and mystery that occurs with atmospheric firing. Wood firing brings to play a deep connection between tending the fire and the work within."
McKenzie Smith

"Square Jar," stoneware, 11" x 8" x 8", wood fired, C. 10. Photo by artist.

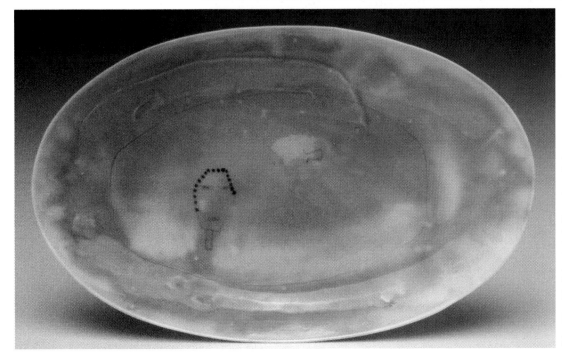

"As I begin to work I have no conscious preconception of the final form. It seems to flow from a silent place deep within me, through my hands, into the clay."
Jill Bonovitz

"Serving Dish," porcelain, 15" x 8.5", hand built, C. 6. Photo by John Carlano.

difficult in art. Not only must the imagery or pattern be arresting in itself (a necessity for any art expression) but this visual information must be orchestrated on the form in an appropriate way.

The relationship between the three-dimensional form and the two-dimensional surface is an essential one. And it is one where a furious visual clash may take place between the form and surface or, conversely, the form and surface may meld together so that one is indistinguishably fused with the other.

Often it is the form of the pot itself that will inspire the ultimate resolution of its surface. Indeed, without form there could be no surface. Leach put it accurately when he said, "Generally speaking, decoration should be subordinate to form but not at the price of dull uniformity. Certain areas of pots call for an accent by banding the articulation of their movement or growth, for example at the neck, shoulder, or just below the major curve. Then the horizontal spaces so formed seem to demand further content."[2] The sensitive, thoughtful potter will be guided by the form itself. Placement

"My majolica is characterized by boldness of color, intricacy of design and elaborate arabesque style."
Rosalie Wynkoop

"Bowl with Tulips," terracotta, 11.5" x 5.5", thrown, majolica, china paint, gold luster, C. 04 and 018. Photo by Josh DeWeese.

"The most beautiful glazes look as if I wasn't there at all, that somehow they just happened as a serendipitous gift of the universe."
John Tilton

"Round Covered Jar", porcelain, 8" x 6" x 6", thrown, soda fired, C. 10-11. Photo by Randy Smith.

"I rely on intuition, spontaneity and what is visceral as a mode creating, and believe that a pot truly reveals itself over time and use."
Fred Johnston

"Zoo Morphic Jug", stoneware, 20" x 10", wheel thrown, wood fired, C.10. Photo by artist.

"Unfortunately, art is too often perceived of as mysterious, elitist, incomprehensible or unimportant. I feel that integrating the handmade object into everyday life is a critical way to access art."

Neil Patterson

"Teapot," stoneware, 5" x 8" x 6", thrown with reed handle. C. 10. Photo by the artist.

of images, pattern and motif can accent or de-emphasize elements already present.

It is also this arena where the idea of dichotomous thinking can once again be put to service. English writer and potter Peter Lane aptly notes, "In general, the more simple the form, the greater complexity of pattern it will support but the emphasis and placement of any pattern is of critical importance."[3] When the pottery form is relatively simple and straightforward, then the surface may carry more intense or energetic visual energy. The expressive character depends upon the relative dissonance or harmony that exists between pottery form and its surface. Emphatic emotions may be portrayed with strong color, pattern and diagonal lines or a somber, quiet mood may be expressed with muted lines coupled with soft, dark, blended pigments.

The very "life fullness" of a pot appears to be manifested in the balance between visual forces that can be considered at odds with each other but are simultaneously unified in the expression. However, any addition to form, whether two-dimensional or three-dimensional, is, at best, no mere appurtenance. Each element of the pottery form is essential to the expressive power of the object.

A lean, hard, symmetrical pottery form may benefit from a surface decoration that undulates rhythmically across its skin. On the other hand, a soft, relaxed, plastic form may be energized with a narrow, tightly thrown cylindrical neck and mouth. Perhaps the surface pattern or image may contradict the form, promoting visual tension, or a motif may loosely embrace the form. And, of course, some pottery may incorporate both kinds of effects simultaneously. The range of possibility is both broad and deep and there can be no suggestion that any expressive limitation exists whatsoever. These surface decoration decisions, like the choice of the pottery form itself, depend upon the mood, character, skills and expressive motives of the potter.

Pictorial imagery may represent much information and narrative while abstract patterns speak to

"My pots are intended to endure as presence visually and physically. Ultimately I want my pots to invite use and demand physical interaction."

Ashley Kim

"Slab Plate," stoneware, 1" x 9" x 6.5", slab construction, salt fired, C. 10. Photo by the artist.

us with a distinctly different voice.

Pattern making has been a hallmark of pottery since ancient times. The regularity of the seasons, day and night, work and rest, life and death permeate life experiences. The patterns that nature presents, whether they are polished pebbles strewn on the beach or the softly bowing grasses of a meadow, contain beauty that cannot be ignored. These patterns can become the impetus for the inspired embellishment of the surface of pottery.

Concerning the importance of pattern, Soetsu Yanagi has said, "Any pattern, if it is a good one, naturally has an element of the grotesque, since it is a reinforcing of beauty—an exaggeration, one might say, without deceit. A pattern, rather than presenting the thing as it is, is a vivid representation of what the thing could never be. Thus, though not a literal depiction, it achieves a verity that transcends realism. Pattern is the power of beauty."[4]

The artist's use of pattern inspired by nature imbues in art a power that springs directly from

"The botanical motifs are not meant to imitate nature, but to evoke it while providing a vehicle to use marks and color in certain rhythms, directions, and arrangements that give meaning and shape to the surface of the specific form."
Linda Arbuckle

"Biscuit Jar: Tall, Hot," terracotta, 8" x 12", wheel thrown, majolica glaze, C. 04. Photo by artist.

nature and life itself. The destiny of the artist, it seems, is to disentangle this mysterious web and present it to the audience in a distilled visual elixir.

For example, in nature, plants bestow a rhythmical profusion of flowing lines, shapes, colors and textures that is inherently visually pleasing. This profusion of characteristics may be incorporated into pottery expressions—but in a more lucid fashion: with pattern. The various kinds of contrasts found within pattern can give movement, life and a poetic truthfulness to the pot.

Thus, pattern making is dependent upon the distillation of the contrasting, elemental formal characteristics that suffuse nature. Through the use of variation, repetition, contrast and other visual tools the potter can cogently express these elements.

But pattern is not a static, lifeless force. It is through the introduction of "irregularity that its life

"The high-fired ash glazes of my pieces reflect natural beauty, such as the minute striations of tree bark and the soft green moss on rocks."
Susan Beecher

"Falling Water Jar", white stoneware, 12" x 6" x 5", thrown, ash glazed, anagama kiln fired, C. 12. Photo by D. James Dee.

"I wanted the finished pieces to work 'in the round,' to carry the audience around and around a particular piece, as many as several times in fact."

Bruce Barry

"Journal Entry #87," stoneware, 11.5" diameter, thrown and altered, mason stains, C. 10. Photo by Dean Powell.

"Creating pottery works which have qualities that enrich the user's life is the ideal and the ultimate goal."

David Crane

"Globe Jar with Barbed Wire," stoneware, 8" x 7", wheel thrown, salt glazed, C. 10. Photo by Tim Barnwell.

fullness is affirmed. This is what the Japanese potter Rosanjin describes as "harmonious discord"[5] that lends balance, unity and life to artistic expression.

Pottery, like three-dimensional sculpture, presents the further opportunity of presenting continuous multiple perspectives by which a pot can be viewed. Thus, the "dimensionality" of the pot must be considered while executing the surface adornment. Unlike a painted canvas, surface imagery in pottery has the ability to begin and end at various points in the three-dimensional composition. For a cylindrical pottery form, a continuous horizontal narration is possible.

For potters, even concepts of horizontal and vertical are inadequate, particularly in reference to imagery placed on the inside or outside surface of a bowl or on the surface of a plate. Potters have devised various strategies to deal with this challenge.

Much of the appreciation of pottery is owed to the tactile circumlocution that is available during handling. A two-dimensional composition residing on the three-dimensional surface of a pot can begin at any place on the form and end at the very same spot. In other words, one may go "full circle" in the appreciation of both form and narration that is presented. For the artist, this

"Ultimately I want the surfaces to seduce the viewer and invite the touch."
Christa Assad

"Coffee Set," white stoneware, 11" x 8" x 4" and 3.5" x 6" x 6", wheel thrown, C. 10. Photo by artist.

"three-dimensional painting" is an exceptionally challenging problem. But when successfully resolved this characteristic of pottery can bring exquisite delight to the viewer/user.

Ultimately, it is the home, after all, for which pottery is made and it is this environment where a relationship with pottery may grow and enrich the life of its user. As Leach has indicated, "One has to live with fine pots in order to appreciate their character, for they are intimate expressions of peoples and their cultures. Human virtues such as nobility, generosity, breadth, simplicity, sincerity and charity—virtues common to both man and pot—are there to be discovered in shape, texture, color and pattern."[6]

[1] McTwigan, Michael, *Surface and Form: A Union of Polarities in Contemporary Ceramics*, p. 4.

[2] From the *The Potter's Challenge*, by Bernard Leach, copyright (c) 1975 by Bernard Leach. Used by permission of Dutton, a division of Penguin Putnam Inc.

[3] Lane, Peter, *Ceramic Form: Design and Decoration*, p. 120.

[4] Yanagi, Soetsu, *The Unknown Craftsman*, p. 115.

[5] Cardozo/Hirano, *Uncommon Clay: the Life and Pottery of Rosanjin*, p. 83.

[6] From the *The Potter's Challenge*, by Bernard Leach, copyright (c) 1975 by Bernard Leach. Used by permission of Dutton, a division of Penguin Putnam Inc.

Sum of the Parts

It is interesting to see an Oriental pick up a pot for examination, and presently carefully turn it over to look at the clay and the form and cutting of the foot. He inspects it as carefully as a banker a doubtful signature—in fact, he is looking for the bonafides of the author. There in the most naked but hidden part of the work he expects to come into closest touch with the character and perception of its maker.[1]

Bernard Leach

"I work under the umbrella of utilitarian potter, exploring and rearranging the boundaries I have set up for what I believe constitutes function."

Jeff Oestreich

"Teabowl," inverted stoneware, 4" x 4" x 4", wheel thrown, impressed decoration, C. 10. Photo by Dan Meyers.

While the overall impact of a pot may be apprehended at once, it may also contain secrets that are only revealed over time. Since the dwelling place of pottery is the home, this intimate daily association with pots can gradually awaken new sentiments long after the thrill of newness has fled. In the best pottery new pleasures, insights, understandings and deeper levels of appreciation of the object may be cultivated on a daily basis.

Some of the unique qualities of the pot, often belatedly divulged, can be found in the transitional essentials of mouth, handle or foot. The attention devoted to these features reflects the care, skill

"My goal in making this work has been to create quiet, simple pots which, like a good meal, leave a healthy, full feeling."
Bede Clark

"Pitcher," stoneware, 9.5" x 5" x 5", thrown, glazed, sand blasted, C. 9. Photo by artist.

and integrity of the maker. A consideration of some of these details may be worthwhile even though an analysis of the individual parts certainly will not constitute the value found in the whole.

At the mouth, or opening, of any pot, the interior volume greets the exterior of the pot. Drinking vessels require a gratifying meeting place for the lips, spouts must pour and, in general, openings need to be comfortably accessible.

Just as an individual's mouth contains a rich tableau of information about the mood of the individual, the opening of a pot can reflect meaningful traits. An inward turning, narrow, pursed termination does much to expressively constrain a vessel form. A portly volume that ends in a restricted opening, or completely covered, can be conducive to a feeling of things withheld or secreted away. A commodious aperture has a more inviting quality. Generosity in circumference speaks to a more extroverted attitude.

For pitchers and other pouring vessels the rim of the pot is a critical transition point. The flared edge of a pitcher may be extended slightly from the body proper or it may more emphatically point the vessel in the direction of its intended use. But its useful role is to deliver, and transfer liquid, all the while making a visual statement.

The spout of teapots and oil dispensers will have a narrowed opening to focus the flow of the stream. The crispness in the manner in which the spout ends often suggests a similar directness in the ending of the flow of liquid during use.

The proportions of these elements, that is, how a particular shape relates to other shapes, can dra-

"I am interested in the way a pot, hand held, seen close up, reveals itself: the rhythms of its making, the character of clay and glazes, the marks of fire, as well as all those subtle modulations of form that give a pot its character, its emotional content and its fitness for use."
Shirley Johnson

"Porcelain Serving Bowl," porcelain, 9" x 3", wheel thrown, gas reduction firing, C. 10. Photo by Peter Lane.

"My forms are spare, with large, simple areas, heavy textures weighty bases, and substantial rims and attachments. I focus on the foot and the rim of a form as the defining elements."

Robert Briscoe

"Oval Casserole," stoneware, 8.5" x 17.5" x 8", thrown and altered, ash glaze, stains, C. 9. Photo by Wayne Torborg.

matically alter the expressive character of a pot. The relationship between the size of foot ring and opening mouth of the pot, for example, can suggest unique and sometimes disparate qualities. And spouts may vary in dimension and scale according to the impression to be made.

The particular shape of the mouth of a pot adds other expressive elements. For example, the ovalized, slightly squared, or out-of-round circle of the mouth of a cup or tea bowl is considerably less formal than the more rigid, consistently circular shape. An undulating lip can add drama to the imperative to drink since options are presented to the placement of one's own lips by the lively edge of the pot.

Technically, it is helpful for utilitarian pots to have the rim or lip slightly fuller than the thickness of the wall for added strength. A beaded edge will be less likely to chip during use.

In addition, different clay types and their related firing temperatures can also dramatically alter the essential characteristics of a pot. For example, earthenware clay may have a slightly heavier wall cross section to compensate for a lack of strength due to its low firing temperature. Stoneware and porcelain, on the other hand, may have thinner walls in cross section, since the fired strength of

"I want my work to touch that distant quiet place in each of us. Balance, home, grace."

Kevin Crow

"Large Teapot," stoneware, 14" x 12" x 10", thrown, raw glazed, wood fired, C. 11. Photo by H. Gentry.

"The work is intended to be whimsical, fanciful, and fun to use."
Shannon Nelson

"Cups and Saucers," white stoneware, 3.25" x 4.75" x .5", thrown, altered and hand built, C. 6. Photo by John Knaub.

these clays is greater. Some potters consistently incorporate a thicker wall cross section to purposefully add strength to a form. This quality will significantly improve a pot's survivability if it is meant for frequent use.

There are as many types of lips, rims and edges to pots as there are pots themselves. In expressive pots, the treatment of the edge of a pot will contribute meaning. The sharp-edged, thin lip of a porcelain cup greets one's own lip with a curt, crisp,

"The family dinner table is the venue of first choice for my pottery."
Joseph Bennion

"Salt Glazed Dish", stoneware, 9" x 5" x 4", thrown and altered, salt glazed, C.11. Photo by artist.

"Our pots are made to be used and enjoyed and hopefully bring a playful elegance to the table."
Karl Kuhns and Debra Parker-Kuhns

"Winged Bowl," porcelain, 7" x 11" x 8", thrown, colored slips, C. 8. Photo by Jeffery Carr.

"I work to find balances between hard and soft, lyrical and angular, masculine and feminine."
Geoffrey Wheeler

"Bowl," porcelain, 8" x 21" x 15", thrown and altered, slab handles, multi fired, C. 6. Photo by Steve Nelson.

"For me the essence of a vessel lies at the threshold where a horizontal curve meets the vertical plane, where thinness and thickness of edges define negative and positive space."
Maren Kloppmann

"Double Stack Box," porcelain, 6" x 5" x 2.5", thrown and altered, residual salt, C. 10. Photo by Peter Lee.

coolness that is significantly different from the soft, rounded, bulbous, and warmer lip of an earthenware mug. The lip of the pot may suggest varied emotions, whether it be turned in or out, thick or thin, squared or round. A pot's lip may be primly circled or sway drunkenly.

This decision to accentuate a particular emotion or idea in any detail of a pot is linked to the artist's sensibilities, skills and the degree of utility desired in the form. A workhorse pot, robustly created for a destiny of toiling day to day, will not have the same characteristics as the more pristine, elegant porcelain form meant for infrequent service.

In addition, with the trend toward a more extensive manipulation of the wheel-thrown cylin-

der, varied shapes such as ovals, squares and asymmetrical forms can be created.

While some pots are perfectly complete without the addition of handles or knobs, these elements are often added to provide further utility and sculptural interest. Handles ease the movement of pottery from place to place, assist in the grasp of the vessel and generally provide efficiency in the tasks set for it. Handles must not only work ergonomically, but also have the additional aesthetic role of extending the lines of the pot sculpturally into space.

Cup handles should display strength and confidence in their role as conveyors of drink. These pottery extensions should be adequately joined to the body of the form as limbs are joined to the body. As potter Linda Christianson has emphasized, there should be a good "marriage" between the two. A handle inadequately attached will be both weak mechanically and aesthetically.

Many tools and techniques can be utilized to make handles. As a result, their shapes are innumerable. Various techniques, including coiling, pulling and press molding, result in shapes easily grasped and lend sculptural embellishment to the overall form.

"My favorite forms are the bowl and cup because these forms are so open and elemental—nothing is hidden."

Gwen Heffner

"Cup and Saucers," porcelain, 5" high, wheel thrown, C. 9. Photo by Ron Forth.

"Each pot holds an exploration of mood, I harmonize the foot of the pot with the rim and the handle with the spout in an attempt to create a unified work."

Simon Levin

"Chubby Pitcher," stoneware, 7.5" x 6" x 6", wheel thrown, wood fired, C. 8. Photo by artist.

But, as Canadian potter Robin Hopper has pointed out, "A badly made handle is a very detrimental detail to any pot, as it is the one part of that pot that is continually in contact with the hand of the user. If it feels inadequate, it will be a constant reminder of its inadequacies. Other details don't have such an intimacy about them except, perhaps, for knobs on lids and the lips on vessels we drink from."[2]

The placement of handles often affects the character of a pot. Symmetrically placed handles or lugs add a sense of calmness or nobility through diametrical balance, whereas a single handle on a teapot or pitcher balances the form in an asymmetrical fashion. Handles can also be made of non-ceramic materials. Twigs, branches, cane and bamboo are standard choices but wire can also strike a strategic expressive blow.

Phillip Rawson says this about handles: "Obviously they are meant for lifting the basic jar: and simple strap-handles meant for just that are very common indeed. But they nearly always develop into a major expressive element in any pottery tradition. Their gestures, proportions, and decorative additions, such as volutes, play a major part in transforming in different ways the basic jars of many different traditions into expressive objects."[3]

The most easily read aspects of pottery form are those that are most obviously presented to the viewer. As a result, the foot of the pot may be mistakenly considered an afterthought or an unimportant element. However, as it is the foundation of the pottery form, the foot determines whether the work stands or falls, both literally and aesthetically.

With pottery, every aspect of form is accessible for inspection and evaluation, including the underside. Without doubt, it is the bottom of the pot where, ironically, the true nature of potter's sensibilities are revealed. Since pottery is an art form whose scale allows close handling, the overall three-dimensional qualities of a pot are critical.

The foot reveals information about the veracity of the maker that cannot be assessed in quite the same way elsewhere in the form. For it is here that the stamina and commitment to craftsmanship and creative thinking are manifested.

Pots thrown on the wheel will normally contain

"No other material or methodology touches my soul more directly than using a pot made out of love and inspiration for the simple task of service with food."
Sandy Simon

"Ice Cream Box," porcelain, 4.5" x 4" x 4", thrown with nichrome wire, C. 8. Photo by Joe Schopplein.

"The inside and underside of a pot are as important to me as the body, handle, spout, lid."
Robbie Lobell

"Soy/Oil Set," white stoneware, wheel thrown, black slip, soda fired with wood, C. 6-8. Photo by artist.

"Each time I sit at the wheel to make a familiar form, I recall the issues raised by the last series of pots I made of that type. How did they look with wider bases? Did I try faceting them? A knob or a handle on a lid?"

Sequoia Miller

"Faceted Footed Bowl," iron rich stoneware, 5" x 11" x 7", thrown and altered, gas reduction, C. 11. Photo by Jay York, courtesy of June Fitzpatrick Gallery.

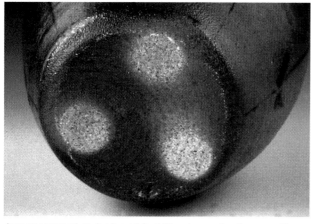

I want my work to look and feel like clay and not some other media."

Larry Davidson

"Vase," stoneware, 5" x 13", thrown, wood fired, shino slip, C. 12+ Photo by artist.

excess clay at the base of the form. The process by which a wheel-thrown pot is trimmed of superfluous weight and the shape defined by a sharpened blade is called turning. But whatever technique is used, whether by cutting, carving, re-throwing, or wire cutting, the way the foot is formed will determine, conclusively, the character of the pot.

Again, Clary Illian speaks eloquently on this aspect of pottery form by saying, "Turning a foot is not just a matter of trimming away unwanted clay

but an opportunity to make a vital, complementary shape that will present the bowl to best advantage. An adequate stem of unworked clay at the base provides the opportunity to make a choice from a variety of shapes and sizes of foot."[4]

The form can be lifted majestically with a tall foot or it may remain squat and stable with a wide treatment. Cutouts to add lift and negative shapes can be carved in the high foot to lighten a top-heavy form. A non-symmetrical foot ring can enhance the overall irregularity of a heavily modeled tea bowl. Feet can also be added by attaching coils or wads of clay to give a sense of three-dimensional space beneath the form as well. This kind of foot can be hand built, thrown or pressed from molds to add distinctive characteristics to the form.

While trimming a thrown form, the act of cutting the clay with a sharp tool reveals the texture and character of the clay. A subtle but significant tactile and visual distinction can be made between this rougher surface, bared while leather hard, to the smoother quality of the rest of the clay that was thrown while plastic and wet. An even more compelling dynamic can be set up by contrasting the rougher, turned foot with the smooth glassy surface of a glaze that descends to meet it. Aside from textural contrasts, other significant contrasts involving color, shape, and movement can be explored in the

"My goal is to integrate form, function and surface in a way that brings a sense of balance and excitement to my work."
Posey Bacopoulos

"Cream and Sugar Set," terracotta, 6" x 11" x 5", thrown and altered, majolica glaze, C. 04. Photo by Kevin Noble.

juxtaposition of elements that comprise the bottom of the pot. A meaningful orbit of delights can be offered at this oft times unexpected juncture.

Like the lip, the foot of the pot is an important meeting place and must be attended to with the same sensitivity, creativity and experience as the seemingly more overt aspects of pottery form.

These transitional elements have distinct roles to play in the success of a pot. Without a lip the pot cannot speak, without a foot it could not stand, and without a handle touch may be lost.

[1] Leach, Bernard, *A Potter's Book*, p. 23.

[2] Hopper, Robin, *Functional Pottery: Form and Aesthetic in Pots of Purpose*, p. 148.

[3] Rawson, Philip, *Ceramics*, p. 98.

[4] Illian, Clary, *The Potter's Workbook*, p. 54.

Mud and Flame

*P*ottery draws on the power of fire, which plays a role far beyond the capabilities of men. Even painted figures or designs on pottery are improved by passing through fire. Pottery has a great advantage in its ability to draw in this way on the power of nature.[1]

Rosanjin

Utilitarian pottery cannot be separated from the primeval forces of nature from which it springs. The primordial elements of clay, water, air, and fire are so taken for granted in modern people's everyday existence as to be forgotten. But for the potter, these staid ingredients are the stuff of everyday magic.

In this sense the potter is a modern alchemist, melding seemingly mundane procedures and mostly unremarkable materials into objects of lasting beauty and value. The transformation of this insignificant material may result in the creation of pottery sometimes deemed priceless.

But pottery ensconced in museums and removed from its utilitarian roots can only be viewed, not touched. With this action an essential dimension of a pot's aesthetic power is lost. But by this incarceration we may be reminded of the true power of nature and the debt owed to her.

While most people readily forget that everything we touch or see around us originates from nature, the potter is constantly reminded of this fact: This mud, this clay, is one of the most common, inexpensive and readily available natural materials known. And the qualities it provides are wondrously appealing: soft, pliable, smooth, and richly variable in color.

In addition, the dichotomous elements implicit in the ceramics process are unmistakable. The potter

"By using a wood flame and natural clays and ashes, I believe there is a possibility of attaining a deeper and more subtle beauty."
Willi Singleton

"Vase," local and commercial clay mix, 8.5" x 7", wheel thrown, ash glazed, wood fired, C. 10. Photo by Scott Berray.

begins with a plastic, malleable material, and the subsequent action of the fire transforms the clay into a rock-hard object that resists even the rigors of centuries.

For pottery, the starting mark is clay. As Leach indicated, "A potter's prime need is good clay. Whether he be industrial, peasant or studio potter the raw material of which pots are made is of fundamental importance. Upon the quality of the clay depends the strength and still more the character of the finished pot."[2]

Indeed, clays available to the potter nowadays have an array of properties. Due to the abundance and availability of raw materials, the potter today can alter and adjust clays in various ways to meet technical or expressive requirements. The initial decision of the type of clay used—earthenware, stoneware, porcelain, and the use to which it will be put—throwing, hand building, faceting, carving, casting, etc.—calibrate the potter's expressive foundation.

The choice of a particular clay dramatically influences the succeeding expressive options of the potter. For example, the color of a transparent or a semi-transparent glaze is significantly affected by

"My goal has been to achieve color in wood firing—colors which combine the conventional wood-fired hues to create surfaces not unlike those found in nature's wildest fauna, flora and oceans!"

Ken Sedberry

"Two Iguanas," custom stoneware, 13" diameter, wheel thrown, wood fired, C. 10. Photo by Tim Barnwell.

"My goal in making functional work is to bridge the gap between elegant china and down-to-earth pottery."

Liz Quackenbush

"Tulip Vase," terracotta, 15" x 4.5" x 9", hand built, Majolica, gold luster, C. 04. Photo by Dick Ackley.

"I intend my pieces to carry life and beauty; I trust they will bring these qualities into the lives of those who use them."
Gay Smith

"Oval Container," porcelain, 8" x 9" x 7", thrown, altered, soda fired, C. 10. Photo by Tom Mills.

"I really hate to cover the beauty of the raw porcelain, so I have worked out some simple glazes that become a skin on the clay."
Gwen Heffner

"Finial Carved Teapot", porcelain, 9" high, thrown, polymer clay finial by Karen Lewis, C. 9. Photo by Mary Resney.

"My clay work is hybridized from many ceramic traditions combining wheel-turned and hand-built construction with narrative painted images that indulge in the pottery form."
Greg Pitts

"Untitled Vase with Pot Tulipiers," white stoneware, 10" high, thrown and altered, C. 10. Photo by Richard Zakin.

the color and character of the clay body beneath it. Interestingly, a single glaze often is not a single specific color. Since glaze and clay fuse in a permanent molten embrace, each suffuses qualities to the other.

Clay, which may be coarse or smooth, light or dark, speckled or pure, plastic or not, will ultimately be a major determinant of the character of the pot. In addition, innumerable colored clay slips, stains and glazes dramatically influence the work of

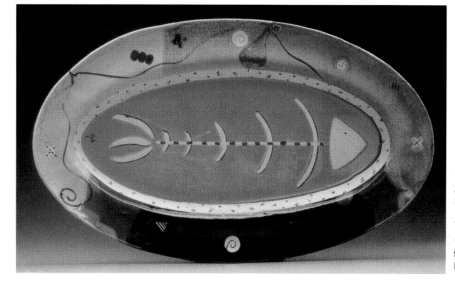

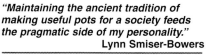

"Maintaining the ancient tradition of making useful pots for a society feeds the pragmatic side of my personality."
Lynn Smiser-Bowers

"Fish bone Platter," porcelain, 13" x 23" x 2", slump-mold slab construction, wax and stencil resist, C. 10. Photo by E. G. Schempt.

the potter.

With minimal preparation, some clays can be used as they emerge from the earth. The natural imperfections of freshly dug clay provide a character all their own. Clay inherently reflects the features of the earth, where rough, cracked, broken, split or textured textures abound. These "natural" qualities of clay can be pursued in their own right to reflect in a direct way those salient features found in the world at large.

Clay, as the foundation upon which all expressive ceramic possibilities rest, determines in a significant way the expressive result. As Philip Rawson has stated, "It is very obvious that some ceramics are made for people who accept clay for what it is—a variety of mud. There is no attempt to hide its affinity with the earth, to transform it beyond the reach of ordinary understanding, or to disguise its surface."[3] Clay—torn, rough, gouged, rent, scratched, slathered, slipped, carved or folded—is a reminder of the surface of the earth and the processes of nature.

This organic quality of clay is often appreciated and exploited by potters. But Frank Lloyd Wright makes an apt comment when he says, "Now there can be no organic architecture where the nature of

"As a potter, my work is implicitly environmental, for the earth under our feet is the material I work with."
Kevin Crowe

"Large Vase," stoneware, 22" x 14", thrown, raw glazed, wood fired, C. 11. Photo by H. Gentry.

"I fire the pots in a wood-burning kiln. The wood firing freckles the pots with ash and flashes the skin of the clay."
Louise Harter

"Wishbone Serving Plate with Wire Mark," stoneware, 2" x 10" x 8", thrown, wood and salt fired, C. 8-10. Photo by Tom Mills.

"The intrinsic beauty of porcelain works well with my affinity toward detail, and they are used together to create a sense of delight and intimacy in my work."
Susan Filley

"Simple Graces," porcelain, 4" x 4" x 3", thrown and altered, copper purple glaze, C. 10. Photo by Tom Mills.

"Would that my pots could talk for me."
Clary Illian

"Vase" porcelain, 16" high, wheel thrown, C. 9. Photo by the artist.

synthetic materials or the nature of natural materials either is ignored or misunderstood. How can there be? Perfect correlation, integration, is life."[4] The incorporation by ceramic artists of these "organic" aspects of clay, fire, water and air into their pottery makes the connection to nature as direct and profound as it can be.

On the other hand, some exquisite pottery is born from a substance that transcends its earthly origins: porcelain. Without a doubt, the fineness, whiteness, purity, hardness and translucency of this "white gold" seems to loom above the foolish play of mortals. In a skilled artist's hands, this material can yield expressions that are the antithesis of mere mud. More difficult to manipulate, dry, and fire, porcelain demands from the potter extraordinary expertise. Because of the technical difficulty encountered at every turn, it is no wonder a certain mystique has arisen around this material.

Rawson notes these expressive extremes inherent in ceramics when he says, "At the opposite pole are those ceramics which attempt to transcend so far as possible the earthy nature of ceramic materials, to make the transformation so extreme that the patron is, metaphorically, removed from all physical contact with the dirty realities of clay making."[5] Porcelain objects have been admired and appreciated for centuries, for their elegance, refinement and rarity. Barring precious metals and stones few materials can surpass, either historically or in modern times, porcelain's appeal.

"The fire is an essential way of marking the surface and transforming the object, giving it life."
Randy Johnston

"Coffee Pot," stoneware, 10" x 8" x 5", wood fired, kaolin slip, C. 10. Photo by Peter Lee.

"I've used no glazes or slips on these pieces, preferring to rely on the vicissitudes of the firing process to texture and color the work."

Jack Troy

"Porcelain Covered Jar," porcelain, 13" high, thrown, ash glaze, anagama fired, C. 9 Photo by Paul Hazi.

From dirt to decorum, the studio potter has a range of expressive options that are as extreme as they are durable.

But the effects wrought by high-temperature firing make the essential transformational process that distinguishes this art form. Dry, unfired clay will crumble willingly and begins to dissolve the instant water greets it. Ceramics, being the art of fired clay, still nestles in the ancient bosom of spark and flame. Without fire, clay is simply squandered.

Modern potters use all available means to produce their ceramic art. But, historically, pottery was fired with solid fuels like wood, charcoal, coal or even dried animal dung. As a result of the use of these solid fuels, the process of turning clay into a ceramic material was an extremely arduous one. With advances in technology, firing ceramics has become much more convenient and less strenuous.

With the advent of natural gas in the late nineteenth century, firing pottery seemed to almost become child's play. As Susan M. Frackleton stated in her book *Tried by Fire*, published in 1886, "All the terrors and mysteries of firing are smoothed away, and all the heavy, dirty, laborious work is no more. Under the present process, whoever can strike the match and turn the gas-tap has sufficient 'force' to fire the china."[6]

More recently, electric kilns have made the firing of pottery even more simple and precise. But this convenience has not come without a cost. As the firing process moves farther away from solid fuels to combustible gas and then to electricity, there is a corresponding decrease in the contributions of the firing process. Solid fuels naturally produce a long tongue of flame that careens its way through the kiln, lashing the pots on its journey to the chimney's exit. This chemically energetic activity can produce varied and exceptional gradations of color, texture, patterning and flashing in the clay and glazes. It is an appreciation of such effects that has inspired renewed interest in this firing method.

Jack Troy, in his book *Wood Fired Stoneware and Porcelain*, writes eloquently on the subject: "There is genuine drama in wood combustion. Years of accumulated tree growth char and unscroll. Suffusing the fire box, roiling flames boost gossamer waves that gather momentum, then feather out beyond the pieces stacked in the first ranks, under the vaulted arch...If the work is tum-

"I try to make strong forms that are receptive to the flame and ash during the four-day wood firing in a Japanese-style anagama kiln."

Randy Edmonson

"Lidded Jar," stoneware, 10" x 8" x 8", thrown, shino glazed, wood fired, C. 12. Photo by Taylor Dabney.

"It is my hope that the viewer/user will be engaged beyond the initial visual impact of shape and color by the subtle mark making resulting from the construction process."
Joan Bruneau

"Pitcher," earthenware, 11" high, thrown and constructed, polychromed glazes, terra sigillata and white slip, C. 04. Photo by artist.

ble stacked, and no shelves employed, the phenomenon is even more dramatic—human activity provokes a flaming wraith, giving it substance and a place to be, in exchange for its heat and mixed blessings."[7]

A wood firing is characterized by an increasing frequency of stoking which raises the temperature of the kiln. Like quickening birth pangs, wood is stoked into the fire box in a accelerating crescendo of heat and flame. Only later, after cooling, is the kiln opened to deliver the fruits of that labor.

In addition, often times during a solid-fuel firing, flying ash will be deposited on the forms, adding further texture, depth and complexity to clay surfaces. Placement of the pots in this type of kiln is critical since some pieces will bear the brunt of the blaze while others will loiter on the sides. In the past, if these effects were not desired, pots were protected from the impinging action of flame and ash by being stacked in clay boxes called saggers.

Additionally, the combustion process produces a chemically altered atmosphere in the kiln because of inefficient consumption of the fuel. Carbon monoxide is generated, producing, with luck, significant and beneficial aesthetic changes in the clay and glazes. This "reduction" in the amount of oxy-

gen available for combustion is a natural consequence of the wood-fire process. Generally, complete combustion of the fuel (oxidation) due to ample amounts of oxygen produces the most efficient firing. But, ironically, it is the inefficient reduction atmosphere that produces such beneficial results at high temperatures.

Firing pottery with combustible vapors like natural gas can produce a similar snake-like flame coursing amongst the pots, but it is not as robust as in a solid fuel-fired kiln. Since the fuel/air mixture can be more readily controlled the results are more even tempered than a solid fuel firing. This approach is more suitable with specific glazes and expressive forms not dependent on the forceful and unpredictable quality of the wood fire.

At the other end of the technological scale is the oxidizing firing of the electric kiln. No combustion occurs and the clay and glazes are simple heated by the radiant energy generated by electricity. Since few aggressive chemical reactions occur, the transformative quality of the firing process is diminished. The clay is vitrified or turned into a tight, glassy matrix and glazes are simply melted. The volatile reaction between clay body and glaze is less dramatic in this type of firing.

On the other hand, the electric kiln eliminates the numerous, unpredictable variables common with wood and gas firings. The artist may concentrate more exclusively on the surface enhancements which often comprise a much more significant aspect of the work. With electric firing, glazes can be more predictable, consistent and brighter.

One can detect an inverse relationship between surface enhancements that are conditional upon the firing method and temperature. While bright, strong and numerous colors can be produced at lower temperatures, the range of colors is narrowed at high temperatures but the richness, depth, subtlety and complexity are more pronounced.

In terms of the unity or balance found in the pot, the artist must select which aspect of the ceramic process will "flesh out" the expressive whole. Some people, as Michael Cardew pointed out, are "mud and water," potters while others are drawn to the flame as the moth is drawn to the light.

Potters today are still discovering the magic inherent in the ceramic process that has remained essentially unchanged from that seminal unremembered, unrecorded moment where mud and flame met ages ago.

"The irregular natural ash glazes of wood-fired work combined with elemental forms provides one evocative means to impel a user into creative collaborations."
Warren Frederick

"Large Platter", stoneware, 2" x 19" diameter, thrown, natural ash glazes, wood fired, C. 10. Photo by Gentry Photographers.

[1] Cardozo/Hirano, *Uncommon Clay: The Life and Pottery of Rosanjin*, p. 79.

[2] Leach, Bernard, *A Potter's Book*, p. 43.

[3] Rawson, Philip, *Ceramics*, p. 12.

[4] Wright, Frank Lloyd, *The Natural House*, p. 24.

[5] Rawson, Philip, *Ceramics*, p. 13.

[6] Donhauser, Paul S., *History of American Ceramics: the Studio Potter*, p. 20.

[7] Troy, Jack, *Wood-Fired Stoneware and Porcelain*, p. 5.

Platescapes

*P*eople content with low-grade tableware can only produce low-grade food. People raised on low-grade food can only become low-grade people.[1]

Rosanjin

"My desire is to bring to life pots that are friendly and intimate, growing ever more personal with daily use."

Malcolm Davis

"Sushi Plate," grolleg porcelain, .75" x 10" x 10", slab built with shino glazes, C. 10. Photo by Dan Meyers.

Bereft of walls, whose interior curvature is slight or sometimes even flat, plates, platters and trays are the stable soldiers of service. These items are stalwart helpers whose functions seem so common as to be ignored. The strength of these forms lies in the subservient role they have been assigned: a platform for the conveyance of food and other items to the table.

But a plate offers more that just this, as critic and writer Vicky Halper explains, "The plate is the potter's canvas, the draftsman's blank page. It is the least specific and the least articulated of the traditional utilitarian forms, and the one most easily adapted for purely aesthetic aims."[2]

The wheel-thrown or hand-built plate is the terrain for the presentation not only of food but also for imaginative artistic pursuits. The plate, as with any other art form, presents its own unique expressive limitations and creative possibilities.

Dualistic principles suggest that since the plate's volumetric qualities are limited, artistic emphasis must be focused on the surface qualities of the

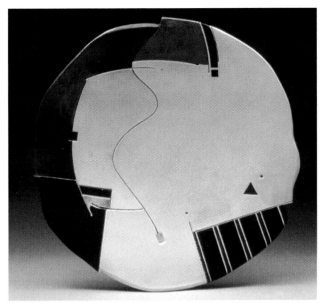

"Plate," white earthenware, 21" x 21" x 2.5", slab construction, underglaze painting, C. 04. Photo by Janet Ryan.

"I see my pottery as portraits of forms that express themselves through use."

Catherine White

"Summer Grass Plates," white stoneware, 1.5" x 8.75" x 8.75", hand-formed slabs, C. 9. Photo by Hubert Gentry.

form. Even though plates are "vertically challenged," they still have a slight, usable volume. However, the subservience of the three-dimensional form to surface characteristics is quite obvious in this pottery type.

Like a blank painter's canvas, plates and trays provide innumerable two-dimensional possibilities to the potter. Painted pictorial decoration as well as pattern making have been the staple of imagery on plates since ancient times and still are viable approaches.

Not only can all the painter's options be embraced, but numerous other ceramic techniques can also be used. As with any other pottery form, the clay can be scratched (sgraffito) while soft and carved when leather hard. In addition, flowing, fluid ash glazes are willing partners of the etched clay surface.

In addition, the fire has its own ability to scorch and flash the surface of these clay canvasses.

Dualistic principles may also be applied to the relationship between a plate's circular shape and the manner in which it is decorated. The circular sym-

"Although the work is not meant to be a literal interpretation of my experiences and ideas, there is a conscious effort to layer my pots with information through the use of pattern, color and form."
Sanam Emami

"Platter," stoneware, 4.5" x 22" x 11, wood/salt fired, C. 10. Photo by artist.

"Changes in my work usually occur without planning things out. I like to let one idea drift into another and see what happens."

Stephen Fabrico

"Platter," stoneware, 22" diameter, wheel thrown, ash glazed, C. 10. Photo by Bob Barret.

figurations—even elevated as when a cake is raised to center stage.

Some potters fill this surface completely with animated images or pattern while others allow the conspicuousness absence of decoration to speak. This, in many ways, is a bolder course of action by the potter.

For some artists, the uninterrupted space of the plate is the foundation for the "main event" which may, in fact, be the food. The plate plays a secondary, supportive role to the drama and artfulness generated during the presentation of a meal. Other potters, meanwhile, see the temporary masking of the plate with food only as a brief interlude that minimally subverts the expressive qualities of the form.

Unlike other kinds of artistic expressions, pottery functions on many different levels. Utilitarian pottery is a balance between aesthetic and utilitarian properties. And various potters stress these different elements of pottery in unique and distinctive ways.

But when these distinctive functions exist they should complement and enhance each other. Just as the flower's comeliness is not hindered by its reproductive function, beautiful pottery is not diminished by its usefulness.

Studio pottery provides for life-sustaining needs, nourishes the soul and provides a livelihood. Unfortunately, vast numbers of the mass-produced objects today fail to meet these objectives.

metrical quality of the form concentrates attention so powerfully that contrasting asymmetrical surface decoration is often times required to produce the requisite dynamic visual interest.

And, of course, the plate does not have to remain round but can come in all shapes and con-

"By reintroducing artistic ware into the home we reconnect art and the everyday."

Simon Levin

"Platter," stoneware, 1.5" x 13" x 6", slab built, wood fired, C. 11. Photo by artist.

Pots function, but they do so much more. The bowl's sensible and sensuous curves, for example, confine potentially renegade food items in a most civilized way. The plate, on the other hand, presents and purveys more docile and less mobile victuals. And the scale of these items, like most usable pottery, is quite small.

These forms cannot be too large since they present particular technical challenges as their size increases. The scale of all ceramic items is limited by the interior volume of the kiln where they are fired. Plates and their kin are no exception to this rule.

Plates and platters normally must have their foot rings firmly on the flat surface of the kiln shelf to minimize distortion or warping during firing. As a result, the size of these forms is limited to the dimensions of the kiln shelves. Since most kiln shelves are not particularly large, it is relatively rare to see a platter form exceeding twenty-four inches in diameter. This is just as well since platters any larger would also be too unwieldy and too heavy for use in any case.

In addition, due to the plate's flat, low shape, it is more prone to cracking during the firing of the kiln than other more upright pots. The thermal shock that is a result of heating pots either too quickly or unevenly can produce a crack known as dunting. Conversely, the plate may crack during cooling as well. This is especially true if cold air is allowed into the kiln as a result of the premature opening of the kiln door. This difficulty is always present in firing any pottery. But plates are more susceptible to this defect due to their shape. The proper management of the kiln during firing is essential if the process is to bear whole fruit.

This firing defect is possible with either thrown or hand-built slab plates, platters, or trays. But the hand-built slab plate presents unique characteristics that are quite distinctive from the wheel-thrown form.

The wheel-made plate is distinguished by the fact that while the expanse of the form radiates out-

"I try to achieve a balance between simple forms and their decorated surfaces, and try to have the pots convey a casual, playful quality."
Stanley Mace Andersen

"Dinnerware," earthenware, 10.75" diameter, thrown, majolica glazed, C. 03. Photo by Tom Mills.

"My cups, bowls, cake platters, and containers, I hope, emphasize the beauty and significance of daily rituals."
Victoria Christen

"Cake Plate," red earthenware, 6" x 12" x 12", hand built with clay slips and underglazes, C. 04. Photo by George Post.

ward, the lip is constantly held in compression during the throwing process. In other words, the form as it extends from the center of the wheel head produces a shape whose outside circumference is continually being "reigned in." As a result, the rim is strengthened and a tight and compact feeling in the overall form results.

In addition, the potter continually supplies water to reduce the friction of the hands against the clay as the form spins on the wheel. As a result, the clay becomes softer and thus less able to retain its shape. Persuading the spinning clay to hold a rela-

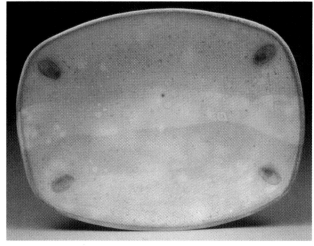

"Softly, the work asks for the viewer's attention. Each piece is ready for a conversation and willing to be part of a greater surrounding."

Matt Kelleher

"Trencher," stoneware, 16" x 11", slab built, soda fired, C. 10. Photo by artist.

"I have been inspired by Japanese Imari ware and its water wheels, star bursts, and other references to daily images."

Richard Hensley

"Platter," porcelain, 2" x 22" diameter, thrown and hand painted, C. 10. Photo by Tim Barnwell.

tively horizontal, cantilevered plane is not an easy task. This is another reason why these forms are demanding.

Plates derived from the slab technique, in contrast, are produced by stretching out the clay, either by hand or by a slab rolling machine, without the corresponding containment action required in wheel technique. As a result, the overall character of the slab is much looser and more irregular. However, just as round plates can be made irregular, perfectly square plates can be made very precisely as well.

Since a flat slab has very little vigor, either structurally or sculpturally, the clay is often draped over a mold while soft so the slight curve strengthens the form as it dries. This curve is sometimes referred to as the "architecture" of the form. Clay forms without at least a minimal curve, whether made from slabs or thrown on the wheel, will often simply "lie down" or slump during the firing, producing a flaccid or failed shape. Strength must be built in from the beginning of the ceramic process.

"I think making pots is like performing alchemy. There's a sense of the miraculous in the transformation of clay from common to precious matter as it endures its trial by fire."

Valerie Metcalfe

"Platter," porcelain, 18" x 3.5", thrown and altered, poured glazes, wax resist, C. 11. Photo by Bruce Spielman.

"I think my best pots are the ones that seem to make themselves, that have so much in them it's like an ambiguous collaboration."

George Parker

"Spiral Plate," earthenware, 26" diameter, thrown, white slip, black stain, C. 05. Photo by artist.

"When the last mark is made and the wheel stops, the pot, like a photograph, captures the dancer in motion."

Michael Smith

"Oval Platter," stoneware, 16" x 12" x 2", thrown and altered, C. 9-10. Photo by artist.

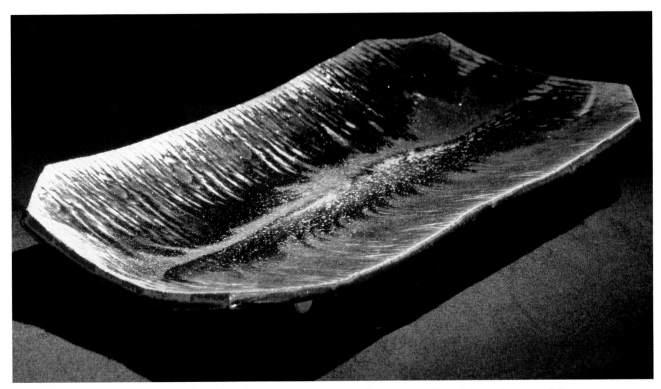

"Making pots is a little like cooking. You have to start with good ingredients to get a flavorful, satisfying result."

Willi Singleton

"Slab Plate," local and commercial clay mix, 20" x 14" x 4", slab built, ash glazes, C. 10. Photo by Scott Berray.

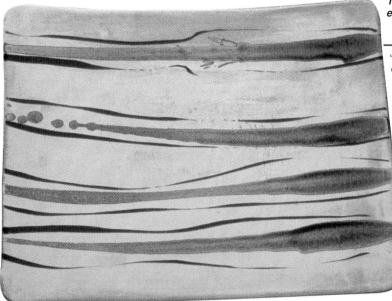

"Rectangular Platter," stoneware, 18" x 14" x 4", slab construction, soda fired, C. 10. Photo by artist.

by utilizing the wood-burning kiln to produce flashing and other surface color and texture irregularities.

Wheel throwing and slab construction can imbue in the plate distinctly different degrees of utility and expressive content. Different aspects of these two processes can also be combined. Some studio potters merge hand-building and throwing techniques to produce distinctive hybrid forms. For example, the thrown plate can be wired off wheel while still plastic and stretched to produce an oval plate instead of a circular shape. And other potters will square the round, wheel-thrown plate by slicing the edges completely away. And organic flat slabs may also be arranged to produce the angular, geometric counterpart to the round plate that springs from the wheel.

In terms of surface treatment, a contrasting, fluid glaze may very effectively compliment the sharp, precise, angular nature of a simple cut slab. Splashed glazes, bold brush marks, spattered patterns or slip-trailed decoration can do much to awaken an otherwise dormant form. The range of expressive possibilities available to enliven the surface of the plate form is too extensive to catalog here.

But it can be shown that there are numerous potters who commit zealously to these forms and devote a large percentage of their creative energies to embellishing this ready and willing surface.

It seems the plate hugs the table's surface in a simple, horizontal gravity-induced embrace. But this useful, humble, recumbent form can be a playful stage where an array of special culinary and aesthetic events occur. Unlike other arenas where food is too often just fuel, provocative dramas can be played out on sensitively wrought ceramic surfaces, thereby bringing meaningful values, sometimes ignored or forgotten, to life.

"I am interested in the lushness and vibrance within nature and the abundant array of forms, shapes, patterns and colors she exudes!"

Susan Sipos

"Nautilus Vegetation Platter," terracotta, 18" x 12", slab built, majolica, C. 03. Photo by artist.

The surface characteristics of a slab of clay are likewise quite different from the wheel-thrown plate. Since the forming technique is one of stretching compared to compression, the personality of the clay is quite different.

Irregular edges, cracks, and miniature fissures arising from this spreading-out process mimic the earthy characteristics found at a macro level in nature. This feeling can be heightened even more

[1] Cardozo/Hirano, *Uncommon Clay: The Life and Pottery of Rosanjin*, p. 125.

[2] Halper, Vicky, *Clay Revisions: Plate, Cup, Vase*, p. 14.

Bowled Over

*I*n a time when we have lost a sense of what endures, of what is primary, the bowl helps us rediscover the roots of pottery, of form. It is the common denominator among forms. It stretches out to make a platter, it narrows to form a vase. It is fundamental, structurally, and helps us see beyond the details that tend to clutter our perception. The bowl helps us to see into the enduring principles of form that will outlast trends and emerge in genuine pots.[1]

Catherine Wright

"Bowls continue as dynamic contributions to an essence of life: Our use of objects as tools to achieve experiences and ideas."
Karen Thuesen Massaro

"Four White Bowls," porcelain, 3.5" x 4" x 5.5", thrown, underglazes, lusters, china paints, C. 9-10. Photo by Paul Schraub.

In terms of the morphology of pottery forms, the bowl precedes practically all others. As one of the most elemental utilitarian pottery forms it is, paradoxically, one of the most subtle and sophisticated. Seemingly mundane, this form is essential for holding foods and other items that are necessary for life. These are basic, wonderful tools.

Ubiquitous to civilized culture, the bowl, with its willing, hollow opening, solves an essentially human conundrum: Containment of food and drink. Conceivably, the inspiration for this utensil came when human hands were first joined in a thirst-quenching gesture.

The ceramic bowl was a dramatic leap forward in surpassing the hands and other less sophisticated

means for producing an efficient gathering place for life-sustaining fare. Also, since the ceramic bowl could be cleaned more readily than other organic utensils, like excavated wooden hollows, it hastened the movement towards a more healthful society.

The availability of clay, the potter's wheel and simple firing technologies put the ceramic bowl within reach of most inhabitants of many cultures.

At first glance, bowls can be considered relatively straightforward since their three-dimensional components are few: Lip, body, and foot. But this form is exceptionally sculptural in character since all parts have spatial implications. The base or the foot is an integral part of the whole and close inspection can yield many clues to the temperament

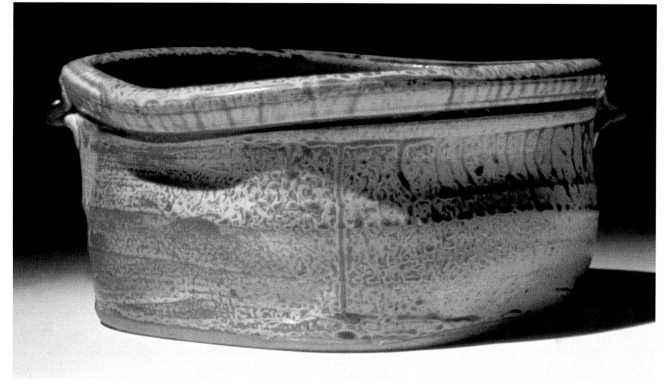

"I avoid formal and elaborate composition and move always toward quiet and subtle simplicity in the pots that I make."
Robert Briscoe

"Crock," stoneware, 5" x 12" x 11.5", thrown and altered, slip, ash glaze, C. 9. Photo by Wayne Torborg.

"I view pottery as a vehicle of hospitality, because a pot gives and receives simultaneously; it is both host and guest."
Silvie Granatelli

"Swan Bowl," porcelain, 10" x 18" x 8", thrown and altered, C. 10. Photo by Tim Barnwell.

"On reflection, the work for the last several years has been dealing with the attempt to transcend and sometimes recapture the earthiness of common clay."
Richard Selfridge

"Quiet Lagoon Teabowl," stoneware with feldspathic stones, 3.25" x 4", thrown, wood fired, C. 11. Photo by artist.

and skill of the potter. The expressive interplay of these basic elements is the sculptural basis of this pottery type.

It is the acquisition of the negative space created by outreaching walls that is the prime utilitarian motivation for this form. And there are numerous kinds of inward or outward, simple or compound curves feasible for the body of the bowl. Each curve or combination of curves makes its own expressive

contribution.

For example, a larger bowl settled on a substantial foot whose girth is much greater than its height provides an arena for an expanded area of visual and useful activity. This kind of form embodies a welcoming, collective gesture, but its weight and scale may inhibit easy handling.

In contrast, the smooth, glossy, petite, soft-lipped bowl is endowed with a more exclusive and personal character since it can be closely handled and may meet the lips with ease. Easily grasped, the small bowl's contours parallel the shape of the hands.

Philip Rawson refers to this particular aspect of pottery when he says, "Since most pots are experienced in use, have been turned this way and that, and seen from many different angles, they have needed to 'work' aesthetically as complete three-dimensional entities. Throughout most of human history they have been felt to inhabit the same world that we as men do, to sit beside us within the reach of our arms."[2] Bowls must pass a close-quarters muster.

Like other pottery forms, bowls can be exquisitely varied and unique. Bowls can be large, small, stemmed, pedestaled, high, low, wide or even narrowed. Bowls can be squared and round, irregular or asymmetric in shape. The lips of bowls may turn inward or flare out aggressively, be beveled parallel with the table surface or dance wobbly above the fray.

"My pots are concerned with utility and the relationship between form and surface. I believe color and surface decoration enhances the simplicity of the form and the transparent glaze allows the "skin" and process to be seen."
Meg Dickerson

"Rice Bowls with Goobers", white stoneware, 7.5" x 11.25" x 8.25", wheel thrown, altered, C. 6. Photo by artist.

"I work because of aesthetic necessity, sharing influences of many times, places, techniques and types of art. I fire my work with wood because of aesthetic choice."

Randy Johnston

"Tripod Bowl," stoneware, 9" high, wood fired, C. 10. Photo by Peter Lee.

In addition, the foot, turned or carved when the pot is leather hard, will have its own character to bestow. The stability and personality of the bowl can be significantly altered by changing the proportions and treatment of this aspect of the form. Low, wide feet imply stability, while a smaller-diameter, taller foot adds an air of grace or perhaps even precarious balance to the form.

Some bowls may be cut off the wheel head with a twisted wire, leaving a regiment of parallel lines to terminate the form. Alternately, bowls may

"I enjoy making bowls because they provide an open, giving presence and an 'inside' and 'outside' challenge."

Don Nakamura

"Bowl," earthenware, 10" x 18" x 18", thrown, underglazes and glazes, C. 05. Photo by Jack Ramsdale.

have feet added that serve to raise the form off the table and give a sense of animal-esque animation to the form. Doubtless, there are an infinite number of possibilities in the interpretation of this particular element of the bowl.

In addition, the basic hollow bowl form can be modified by additions for different purposes. Handles can be attached to make cups, lids can be added to complete covered jars, scale can be increased to make large basins and punch bowls or bowls may be tamped down so they approach the platter form. The variations are so rich and diverse that it is sometimes difficult to determine whether, indeed, a bowl is a bowl is a bowl.

A further attraction to this form makes it unique in the morphology of pottery: both inside and outside are accessible in every way. Unlike practically every other kind of pot, the bowl's entire skin is available for the artist's exploitation and the user's scrutiny. Interior and exterior are both equal and accessible.

Varied combinations of images, patterns, textures or motifs can meander throughout the interior and exterior of the form. These two-dimensional elaborations can be related intimately by joining the surfaces in harmonic interplay or they can be used as foils to contrast visual elements in a dynamic way. Visual games of all sorts can be played on either inside or outside or both surfaces of the bowl.

The interior portion of the bowl may itself be used to express unique ideas and allusions as well. This breach can suggest elements found in the earth's landscape such as the hollows, depressions, craters and basins.

And when food is placed into it this space it can become a metaphorical landscape. A bowl can be transformed into a pond with carroted islands, a noodled sargasso sea, or a cresting mountain of potatoes.

And much like the landscape, a bowl's continuous curves imply a sense of the infinite. As writer and critic Michael McTwigan stated, "In addition to being eminently practical, the potter's plate and bowl present us with an unending horizon; no corners trap the eye, or the soul."[3]

Certainly the potter's wheel is an agreeable instrument for the creation of bowls. They appear to spring naturally from the potter's fingertips since the laws of physics lend a helping hand. Centrifugal force aids the potter by naturally expanding the spinning clay from the upstart cylinder towards an ever-widening circle. Just as we feel pulled to the outside edge of the merry-go-round, so too is clay led in this outward direction.

Gravity, on the other hand, is not pulling out

"A pot positions itself within the order and function of a living space through imagination and use. There, it does not come to rest, but continuously stirs."

Linda Sikora

"Server on Stand," porcelain, 5" x 9" x 7.5", thrown, wood/oil/salt fired, C. 10. Photo by Peter Lee.

but down, and needs to be countered at every turn by the potter. Barring the slightest misjudgment in handling these forces, the potter arrives at a bowl in a surprisingly quick fashion.

But during throwing, the more horizontal the deflection of the wall, the more likely the form will collapse, since the force of gravity always acts upon the soft, spinning, wet clay. This is especially true for low, wide shapes with a narrow foot circumference.

Clary Illian explains this further in regard to bowls by saying, "Because the clay is cantilevered out from a narrow base, gravity, always the potter's enemy, becomes an even greater factor, and bowls cannot be fussed over. They must be made with economy of movement and time. Even more than in the throwing of cylinders, each movement can sabotage the next."[4] Skill, craftsmanship and vision are tested, surprisingly, in the production of this humble vessel.

In addition, the presence of the potter's throwing rings, purposeful perturbations or serendipitous irregularities in the wall of the

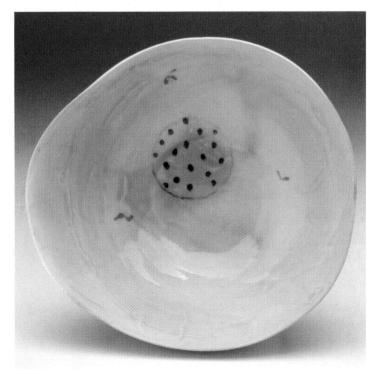

"I like to think of my work as quietly infused with meaning."

Jill Bonovitz

"Bowl," porcelain, 7" diameter, hand built, C. 6. Photo by John Carlano.

"Through minimal expression of form and surface, I intend to extend the notion of functional containment to that of sculptural presence."

Maren Kloppman

"Untitled", porcelain, 16" x 7", coil built, soda fired, C. 10. Photo by Peter Lee.

"The intimate relationship between maker and object solidifies with each fired piece, giving rise to a functional object that freely conveys 'my bliss' to the user."

Kate Maury

"Bowl," porcelain, 13" diameter, wheel thrown, soda fired, C. 10. Photo by Bill Wikrent.

pot can offer a rich array of sensory information to the hand. The texture of the glaze, both to the touch of the hand and the lips, is a critical element in the aesthetic appreciation of this form. And, of course, weight in relation to size adds to the aesthetic dynamic when a bowl is lifted.

In our own culture people may find various values to be important in their own appreciation of pottery. For some it may be bright colors and pattern, for others neutral, subdued tones. Particular or peculiar shapes may cast a spell. But, without doubt, the tactile quality of a bowl is one of the defining elements of this form.

Rosanjin, a Japanese potter, says, "For any two pieces of pottery, the form and design may be the same, but the inner spirit is always different. And in analyzing the inner spirit of various works, one discovers qualities whose superiority is intrinsic and others whose superiority is extrinsic. The presence of these in varying degrees, each combination yielding its own result in a different form, accounts for the amazing range in value."[5]

Even after all these centuries, today's potters are exploring the aesthetic possibilities inherent in this fundamental, necessary form. Hand-made bowls reflect the idea that there are important, long-lasting values associated with the most basic activities in our daily lives. And the bowl punctuates these activities, in a myriad ways: Some mindful at times, while at other times, half remembered or even forgotten.

"My aim is to make pots that sing of their nature in a total way. In rim, foot, surface and form...a common language...a single voice."

Ellen Shankin

"Boat Bowl," stoneware, 6" x 14" x 7", thrown and assembled, C. 9. Photo by Tim Barnwell.

"The form or shape of the work is my primary interest outside of utility."

William Brouillard

"Ice Cream Bowls," porcelain, 4" x 6" x 3", wheel thrown, C. 10. Photo by artist.

"I am interested in the animation of form and how the use of decoration can accentuate that movement."

Kate Inskeep

"Bowl," porcelain, 13" diameter, thrown, slip, soda ash, wood ash, C. 10. Photo by Pat Minniear.

"The majolica technique provides me not only with a wide range of bright, sharp colors to use in developing the patterns and designs I paint on my pots, but also allows me more freedom and control over my treatment of the surfaces."

Stanley Mace Andersen

"Mixing Bowl," earthenware, 5.5" x 12", wheel thrown, majolica glazed, C. 03. Photo by Tom Mills.

"I value the challenge that comes with making utilitarian objects that strive to engage and inspire."

Michael Kline

"Set of Bowls," stoneware, 7.5" x 7.5" x 5.5", thrown, hakeme brush work, vine brush work, salt glazed, C. 10. Photo by Walker Montgomery.

---

[1] Wright, Catherine, "*Studio Potter*, "The Bones of the Bowl," Vol. 1.

[2] Rawson, Philip, *Ceramics*, p. 91.

[3] McTwigan, Michael, *Surface and Form: A Union of Polarities in Contemporary Ceramics*, p. 6.

[4] Illian, Clary, *A Potter's Workbook*, p. 49.

[5] Cardozo/Hirano, *Uncommon Clay: the Life and Pottery of Rosanjin*, p. 77.

Lip Sync

*B*ut the important question is how in our disinte-
grating times individual potters are to discover
their particular kind of truth, in other words, their
highest standard, and further, by what means it can be
passed on to other artist-potters to the end that
humanistic work of true merit, especially for domestic
use, may be produced.[1]

Bernard Leach

"How can you adequately describe the touch of a lip to the edge of a cup, or the way a brush mark can convey energy or symbolize a flower or provide a blush of color that sets apart one space on a form from another?"

Wayne Branum

"Cups," stoneware, 3" x 3" x 3.5", wheel thrown, C. 9-10. Photo by Peter Lee.

It is necessary to drink liquids daily to sustain life. The frequent contact with drinking vessels of all types is unavoidable.

Cup, mug, tankard, tumbler, demitasse, chalice and goblet—all have the duty of transferring liquids from one point to another. And what an important and sensitive destination it is! These ceramic creations must not only please the eye and the hand, but also one of the most intimate and sensitive features of human anatomy: the lips.

This aspect of human anatomy is a critically important in so many different ways. The spoken word emanates from the lips. The expression of love and passion is directly associated with the lips. From Christians to Zen Buddhists, the imbibing of liquids signifies spiritual, life-sustaining references and meanings. In addition, one's own personal physical health is determined by the consumption of food and drink that pass this fleshy portal.

Pottery, in general, is closely associated with essential processes of life. But drinking vessels are inseparable partners in the maintenance of human health. Since the intermediary destination of life-sustaining nourishment is the mouth—sensitivity to ing with any other medium have this challenge placed before them.

Heavy and hulking or light and graceful, each kind of ceramic cup lends its own character in the enjoyment of liquid refreshment. These small beverage containers have significant limits in shape or design but are unequivocal in their function. All liquid refreshment needs a transfer container and the potter's cup or mug aims to satisfy—beautifully.

Strictly speaking, thirst can be quenched effortlessly by the cupped hand—efficient, effortless and always available. And a plain cylindrical vessel will certainly suffice. However, humans seek more than just an efficient tool. Herein lies the aesthetic challenge of this type of ceramic form: How does the potter invest something important, lasting, and significant in such a seemingly simple, straightforward form?

"I use nature as a source of inspiration..."
Larry Davidson

"Cup," stoneware, 4.25" x 4", thrown, wood fired, C. 12+. Photo by artist.

this aspect of the drinking vessel is an essential concern of the potter.

Certainly, for artists it is important to please the eye and to engage the mind. And for craft artists it is necessary to enlighten the hand. But it is the potter who must also delight the lips. Few artists work-

"This is what inspires me: For many years I have been looking for a way to combine drawing and ceramics, and on a greater scale, art and technique. I am excited by, and feel drawn to, each, and cannot separate them in my work or life."
Ann Tubbs

"Face Mug," red stoneware, 3.5" x 5", wheel thrown, pulled handle, C. 3. Photo by Jerry Anthony.

Since the cup form lacks sculptural complexity, the potter must find expressive potential in the forming technique, by incorporating surface imagery/pattern or by a unique combination of the relatively direct elements that comprise the overall form. For the potter, the aesthetic choices found within the drinking vessel exist in a narrow range but, paradoxically, are remarkably deep.

In making cups, the type of clay the potter chooses focuses the character of the expression. This choice frames the artistic decisions to follow

"I want my pots to be soft to the drinker's lip, to be secure in the pourer's grasp, and actively to thrill the touch of those who set their table."
Cheri Long

"Three Whiskey Bottles," stoneware, 6" tall, wheel thrown, wood and salt fired, C. 6. Photo by artist.

"The essence of making pots for me is about being human. It's about fragility and strength. It's about the intimate moment when the handle of a cup touches the hand."

Chris Staley

"Four Cups," stoneware, 10" x 12", wheel thrown and hand built, C. 6. Photo by the artist.

"The pots I make are to be used. Their form and glaze are to be inviting, comfortable to the touch and to compliment what is be contained."

Jess Parker

"Lidded Cups", porcelain, 5" x 5", wheel thrown, soda fired, C. 10. Photo by artist.

since the properties of the clay bring to the expression particular qualities.

Porcelain, the purest of clays, provides a blank white canvas on which subtle glazes or graphic imagery may be placed. Due to its whiteness, porcelain usually tends to lie on the cool side of the emotional spectrum. This is ironic, considering the very high temperature necessary to vitrify porcelain.

After firing, porcelain is a very dense, hard and glass-like material. As a result of this density, the transference of heat from cup to the hand is rapid and direct. For this reason a porcelain cup or mug, if used for hot beverages, requires a handle. This is a rich avenue for exploration since a wide variety of possibilities exist in technique, form and placement of this appendage.

Stoneware clay, on the other hand, contains a

relatively small but significant percentage of iron oxide that produces innumerable colors (depending upon the type of firing). As a result of the fluxing action of iron, the clay fires to a hard, dense consistency that, like porcelain, also transfers heat quite readily. But the presence of iron in this clay produces a much warmer, softer and variegated texture. Depending upon the firing, the fluxed iron will sometimes bleed through the glaze to produce a rich, mottled and pleasing pattern.

Like blood brothers, stoneware and porcelain are different in character but similar in spirit.

By contrast, red earthenware clay cannot be vitrified. That is, it cannot be transformed into a tight, dense, glassy matrix by the action of the fire. This is due to the presence of a relatively high percentage of iron oxide. Because of this, an earthenware clay

"I recognize an inherent beauty in pots based on their relationship to human need and their potential for making human connections."

Todd Wahlstrom

"Cup and Saucer," porcelain, 4" x 5", thrown, slip decorated, C. 10. Photo by artist.

"Making a simple coffee mug comes from my desire to enjoy the practical use of an object from which emerges a seductive aesthetic voice."

Stephen Godfrey

"Coffee Mugs," porcelain, 4" x 3" x 3", thrown and altered, soda fired, C. 10. Photo by artist.

"I typically choose high fire clay and glazes for the burned and melted qualities often evident."

Christa Assad

"Cups," stoneware, 4" x 2.5", wheel thrown, C. 10. Photo by artist.

body will remain somewhat porous after the firing. Consequently, earthenware objects tend to insulate the heat of the beverage from the touch from the hands. This is especially true if the wall cross section of the earthenware cup is fairly thick. This is quite normal for earthenware objects since greater strength cannot be derived from the firing process. However, due to the more porous nature of earthenware clay, the thicker wall cross section will not necessarily translate into heavier weight.

In addition, potters today are not limited to just red earthenware clay. A rich variety of white, orange, brown and colored clays are available in this low temperature range that produce quite diverse and interesting affects.

"My hope is that my pots invite use and that my pleasure in making them is shared by those who use them."

Posey Bacopoulos

"Cup," terracotta, 4.5" x 5" x 3", thrown and altered, majolica glaze, C. 04. Photo by D. James Dee.

"Our goal in this body of work is to produce objects that reach an audience that is concerned with beauty in everyday life."

Bruce Winn and Michael Roseberry

"Untitled," porcelain, 5.5" x 3" x 3", slab built, C. 6. Photo by artists.

Following the choice of a clay body, the straightforward elements of lip, body, foot and possibly handle will naturally occupy the potter.

In particular, the relative thickness of the cup's lip, whether deflected inward or turned outward, and the undulation or irregularity of the open circumference will help to determine the cup's overall usefulness and expressive character. Squared mouths, ovalized openings and even serpentine meanders of the lip can add interest and character to the vessel.

The lip of the cup, however, must be carefully considered by the potter lest a negative experience spoil the entire aesthetic of the form. A thicker lip is certainly more appropriate for a beer stein found in a more tumultuous setting than a demitasse cup conceived for a more tempered environment.

There also needs to be ample volume provided to hold an appropriate amount of liquid. The overall shape and size of the form itself depends upon the nature of the refreshment and the skills and imagination of the potter.

Various indentations or textures and pronounced throwing rings or ridges can produce graspable areas that can make the form a comfort in the hand.

All the physical characteristics manifested in the ceramic drinking vessel must by unified by the expressive intent of the artist. Robust or delicate, black or white, heavily textured or smooth, porcelain or earthenware, narrative imagery or pattern are all choices the potter makes to instill in the work a particular emotional feeling or intellectual idea. By doing this, a part of the artist is made permanent and irreducible by the action of the fire.

Although ceramic drinking vessels have been made by people of many cultures, the sensitivity towards the drinking vessel is probably best exemplified by oriental potters. For some in the Japanese

"These are forms and surfaces which I never grow tired of. They are rooted in ceramic history, yet, I hope they reflect a personal and individual quality of feeling."
Bede Clarke

"Cup," stoneware, 4" x 3" x 3", wheel thrown, wood fired, C. 12. Photo by artist.

"The wood-fired stoneware are special pots that have 'been somewhere'—they have experienced an extreme assault of ash and flame, a thermal wind that decorates them with scars and blushes where they have been touched by nature."
Richard Selfridge

"Bizen Style Tea Bowl," stoneware with feldspathic stones, 5.5" x 3.5", wheel thrown, wood fired, C. 12. Photo by artist.

culture this seemingly mundane utensil has been elevated to rarefied heights. In Japan the tea bowl form springs from a tradition of handleless cups and, as a result, can be considered a shape archetype. An indispensable part of the centuries-old Zen Buddhist tea ceremony tradition, the tea bowl reflects a level of sophistication and connoisseurship unrivaled elsewhere.

For example a tea bowl's shape may be related directly to the seasons. The more narrow, cylindrically oriented winter tea bowl, with its restricted opening, will lessen the evaporation of hot tea. As a result, the warmth of the beverage will be retained for a longer period of time. This is a most appro-

priate quality for a drinking vessel used in the winter months.

On the other hand, the summer tea bowl, shorter and larger in diameter with a correspondingly wider mouth, accelerates the cooling of the tea.

In addition, the surface characteristics and glaze affects of these tea bowls reflect a rustic beauty that incorporates the richness and complexity of nature. As a result of the power of these objects, many Western potters have been inspired to echo similar concerns in their work.

Minnesota potters, in particular, create a more versatile version of this type of handleless ware that is not generally associated with the tea ceremony (and are more likely used for the drinking of spirits rather than tea). They are referred to by the Japanese term "yunomi" and come in a broad range of styles and forms.

In the West the demand for traditional-style Japanese tea ceremony tea bowls, sans handles, is limited. However, coffee cups with handles certain-

"Being fond of glaze and not willing to give up this surface altogether, I play with the relation of glaze to clay surface."
Jeff Oestreich

"Tea bowls," stoneware, 4" x 4" x 4", wheel thrown, faceted, wax resist, salt glazed, C. 10. Photo by artist.

ly have a broader appeal.

The first requirement for this type of form is a handle comfortably and securely attached to the form. Balance, leverage, strength, and tactile qualities of the handle are primary considerations. In addition, the curve or angle that comprise the handle's shape also should agree with the body and reflect the transitional feeling the artist deems appropriate.

The surface resolution of the cup form is of utmost importance as well. A good fit between the clay body and glaze is essential so that each reflects well on the other and contributes further strength to the form. And, of course, these kinds of elaborations can take on pictorial form and become an essential visual attribute.

Stemmed cups, such as goblets and taller drinking vessels like tumblers, present their own unique set of issues, including stability and integration of the varied three-dimensional and two-dimensional elements.

The drinking vessel is comprised of a few seemingly unexceptional parts. But each aspect of the cup form becomes remarkably important since so much of the aesthetic success of the object depends upon these fundamental parts. Simple and straightforward aspects of the pot—lip, body, foot, handle and surface elements—must all work harmoniously and contribute distinctive qualities for this type of ceramic form to succeed as a work of art and as a useful drinking vessel.

A favorite cup, perhaps first selected for its pleasing visual and tactile elements, becomes even more special as time passes. A visceral familiarity with the item is acquired by daily experiences. A ceramic cup incorporating endearing intimate, tactile, and visual qualities brimming with a favored beverage can produce a sense of calming connection to everyday experiences.

A handmade cup or mug meant for service cannot succeed solely as a utilitarian object. It must convey the spark of life that distinguishes all genuine artistic expression from the merely manufactured.

This is one of the things that pottery does best, that is, freeze in a moment of time a living gesture that springs from the head and heart through the artist-potter's hands and to the table. Raise your handmade cup high! Cheers! Prost! Skoal! Salute!

"Perhaps some of the best attributes of contemporary pottery can only be revealed through daily use."
Linda Christianson

"Cup," stoneware, 5" x 5" x 4", thrown, wood fired, salted, C. 10. Photo by artist.

"The knowledge that my pots have purpose and these past traditions are carried forward reinforces my belief that making pots is a great way to spend the day."
Lynn Smiser Bowers

"Twin Mugs," porcelain, 4" x 4" x 3", wheel thrown, pulled handles, reduction glazes, C. 10. Photo by E.G. Schempf.

"I'm intrigued by what happens when clay is rolled, stretched, pressed, incised, inlaid, extruded, bent, cut and put back together."
D. Hayne Bayless

"Four Tumblers," stoneware, 7" tall, hand built, C. 10. Photo by artist.

---

[1] Leach Bernard, *A Potter's Book*, p. 15.

Bottled Up

*W*hy do we long for beauty? The Buddhists would
reply that the world of beauty is our home and
that we are born with a love for home. To long for
beauty, therefore, is the same as to long for home.[1]
Soetsu Yanagi

Many utensils are necessary for the complete and proper functioning of the home. Historically, it has been the potter's task to create useful and beautiful items to satisfy those
domestic needs. Many diverse types of ceramic forms have
been created but it is the bottle's job to contain and control
liquids. Unlike teapots and pitchers, whose primary purpose is
to dispense liquids, vases and bottles generally have three possible functions: Pouring, storage and display.

Indeed, a bottle or vase essentially is a utensil whose
design is to bring liquids to heel.   Fortunately, liquids con-
form to the shapes in which they are placed. Therefore,
the range of expressive possibilities for bottle, vase
and decanter forms is immense.

Most of these constricted ceramic forms are
devoted to the serving, storage and presentation of various liquids. But the fundamental
substance is water. Basically, the potter must
heed the qualities of this material:
Liquidity, pourability, evaporative tendency
and shapelessness. The implications that
spring from these characteristics have formal consequences for the potter in creating
this particular type of ceramic utensil.

"Function is a condition of the pots I make."
Linda Sikora

"Vase," porcelain, 11" high, thrown, resist glazing, wood-oil-salt fired,
C. 10. Photo by Peter Lee..

Water, after all, is an ephemeral material. Therefore, the narrowed neck of the vase or bottle form acts as a conservation measure; reducing the surface area available for evaporation. Without this narrowed opening any liquid would quickly disappear. The narrow neck of the bottle, also serving as a spout, constricts the flow of liquid, producing a forceful poured stream. In the case of the decanter, the neck simultaneously acts as spout and handle. A further advantage of the constricted opening is that it can be conveniently capped or plugged, further reducing evaporation and protecting the contents from contamination.

Generally, vases and bottles are small in scale and are composed of the straightforward elements of lip, neck, body and foot. The principal distinction of this form is obviously the narrowed elongation that comprises the neck of the form in contrast to the usually bulbous lower reservoir.

It is the relationship between these two basic form elements that presents the potter with an exquisite opportunity for expressive possibilities. The integration of these distinctive parts can produce an exciting and provocative range of a shape

"It's a huge challenge to stay within the confines of function, with all its millennia of tradition, and still express something personal."

Lisa Naples

"Bottle Neck Bud Vase", earthenware, 8" x 6" x 2", slab built, slips, glaze, C. 04. Photo by James Quale.

"I try to instill my pots with a sense of gesture and generosity that not only invites their use, but almost seems to anticipate it."

Thomas Rohr

"Whiskey Bottle with Cup," porcelain, 14" x 4", wheel thrown, wood fired, C. 12. Photo by artist.

"I strive constantly to put life and movement in each piece, through manipulation and carving as well as in creating and choosing unique glazes which fit the form."

Ian Stainton

"Vase," porcelain, 10" x 7", thrown, altered, carved, C. 10. Photo by Bruce Cramer.

and volume possibilities. While these shapes may terminate abruptly or merge gracefully, the relationship between them determines the overall quality to be found in the whole.

The affect found in an abrupt termination between the neck and body is based upon contrast instead of smooth continuity. The expressive content of this type of form is focused in competing visual interests generated by the consequences of joining seemingly disparate visual elements. The nearly vertical straight line of the neck of a bottle meeting the fullness of the body joins the two elements in an interlocking play of form contrasts. This aspect alone constitutes a visually dynamic affect.

In addition, the extension of the neck of the bottle also has strong masculine anthropomorphic implications while, conversely, the full bulbous quality of the body of the form hints at the feminine realm. The unification of these dualistic characteristics in one expression may add a subliminal element to the allure of this particular ceramic form.

Without doubt, the lip and foot can add their own sculptural statements in regard to lift, movement, or stability. Like the example of a ballerina, the grace of a tall, sinuous bottle can be enhanced with the incorporation of a proportionately smaller foot. But as the foot diameter becomes smaller there is a corresponding loss of stability and therefore, utility. Alternately, the lift of the bottle can be

"If serendipitous events enliven my work, they result from my devotion to both care and prayer."

Jack Troy

"Paddled Porcelain Bottle," porcelain, 11" high, thrown, paddled, anagama fired, C. 9. Photo by Hubert Gentry.

"My intent as a potter is to make pots that embrace the functional aspects of our lives while yet transcending them."
James Sankowski

"Vase," white stoneware, 19" x 7.5", thrown and altered, slip trailed, C. 10. Photo by Stanley Blanchard.

"Our objective in potting is to facilitate a seamless relationship between clay, glaze, fire, hand and mind."
Will Ruggles and Douglass Rankin

"Oval Bottle," stoneware, 7" high, thrown and paddled, wood fired with salt and soda, C. 9. Photo by Will Ruggles.

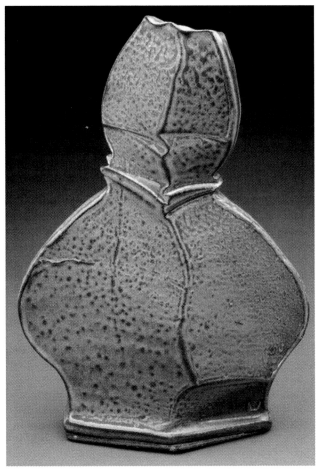

"My work is a fusion of intent and improvisation."
Brad Schwieger

"Cut Vase," stoneware, 17" x 11" x 4", thrown and altered, soda fired, C. 10. Photo by artist.

"Pots offer a uniquely human connection, for they are an inevitable extension of the potter's hands, inner force and sense of beauty."
Gwen Heffner

"Patterns of Washi Paper," porcelain, 11" high, thrown, paddled, carved, C. 9. Photo by Geoff Carr.

further emphasized by turning the opening or mouth upward. On the other hand, by flattening the flare of the lip the vertical emphasis can be given a horizontal heading, thus giving an earthy direction to a form that aspires to the heavens.

As can be seen time and time again, the manipulation of particular formal elements of a pot can dramatically alter the expressive content of the object. Proportional dissimilarities emphasize different elements of the object, giving power to one, often at the expense of another. In so doing, the potter manipulates the emotional weight, significance and meaning with these elements.

Interestingly, it is through the alteration of one of the basic elements of the bottle's morphology that the vase comes into being as a distinct class of

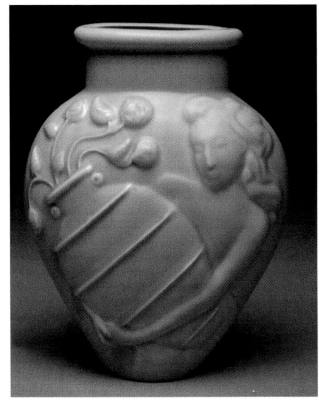

"The function of pottery is integral to its design in spite of its sculptural, decorative, and symbolic elements."
Donna Polseno

"Vase," porcelain, slip cast, C. 7. Photo by Tim Barnwell.

"I enjoy presenting my work so that a viewer might notice and appreciate subtle diversities in form and surface."
Jason Hess

"Seven Tall Bottles," stoneware, 18" x 3.5" x 3.5", thrown, wood fired, C. 11. Photo by artist.

"My pottery is a reflection of an interest in history, gesture, architecture and function. The pots also reflect my interest in the forms and patterns found in the natural world."
Michael Kline

"Jardiniere," stoneware, 18" x 10" x 10", thrown and altered, underglaze, wax resist, wood fired, C. 10. Photo by Walker Montgomery.

ceramic objects. It is simply the enlargement of the neck of the bottle that produces what some might consider the stereotypical vase. That is, a closer volume relationship exists between the body and neck of the vase form, whereas the bottle form relies on the proportional divergence between the body and neck of the pot.

Unlike the bottle, which has more than one function, the vase is used almost exclusively for the presentation of flowers or other natural objects. Without vases, the presentation of beautiful things from nature would be lost to us.

The longing to bring aspects of the natural world into our living spaces has existed in many cultures for centuries. The appreciation of the special beauty of the reproductive organs of various plants may be considered a universal human trait. In Western cultural these plants play a significant role in the many important aspects of life, including the celebration or commemoration of significant social events, including romance, birth, anniversary, birthdays, and death.

It is hardly surprising that the power of nature's beauty has historically inspired artists.

The vase form, tapped to compliment the samplings of beauty from nature, has been evolving for centuries. In China, a certain style of pot called the mei-ping vase was utilized expressly for the display of the plum or prunus blossom branch. In many respects, this historic ceramic form, due to its elegant and austere shape and volume, could be considered "classical".

This ancient interest in and appreciation of flowers has continued to the present. In particular, the Oriental art of flower arrangement known as ikebana has generated a growing number of devotees in the West. The evolution of this particular art form has done much to change the physical and proportional parameters of the vase form.

Typically, the constriction of the neck of such forms allows the presentation of nature's beauty by providing a narrowed opening in which the stems of the flowers are held upright. The bulbous portion allows for the continued liquid nourishment of those visual delicacies for an extra moment in time. These two aspects of the vase form have been the basis for the innumerable permutations of form explored by potters past and present.

But since there is so much freedom today considering the kind of floral compositions and pottery possible, it is not surprising that the ceramic containers have also changed in significant ways.

Multiple openings and clever strategies for keeping the stems of flowers erect have also been employed. As Robin Hopper has indicated, "In upright forms of traditional Japanese vases, there is often a scratching of the inner surface of the top inch or two to allow wooden or twig cross pieces to be wedged in to hold the flowers."[2] The contempo-

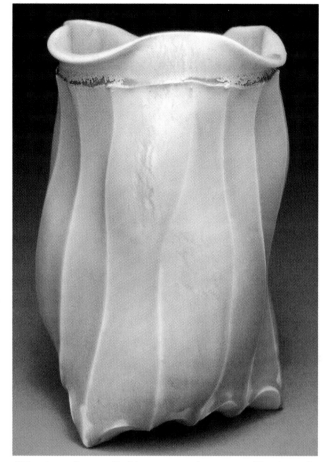

"Directness is a quality I hope my work conveys. Directness is related to how I use the ceramic process. It results from making a pot that grows from the process naturally—comfortably."
Aysha Peltz

"Vase," porcelain, 8.5" x 5", wheel thrown and altered, C. 10. Photo by Todd Wahlstrom.

"I make pots which incorporate decoration, ornamentation, and a playful sense of humor within the context of function."
Susan O'Brien

"Flower Brick," white stoneware, 12" x 12" x 10", wheel thrown, hand built, luster, C. 10. Photo by artist.

"Flower Brick," terracotta, 11" long, thrown, manipulated, reconstructed, sgrafitto, C. 04. Photo by Erma Estwick.

"Colfax Vase," stoneware, 7" high, thrown and hand built, salt glazed, C. 10. Photo by Joseph Gruber.

rary Western flower brick accomplishes the same purpose but the lattice opening becomes part of the overall composition of the pot.

Most individuals would consider the vase as having a vertical axis. However, depending upon the requirements of the particular floral arrangement, the vase can be oriented on the horizontal as well. For that matter, the interplay between pot and flower can be a dynamic one with the pottery form influencing the nature of the floral composition and vice versa.

The exterior of the bottle or vase form is also one where numerous strategies have been employed by the potter to add delight to the form. The verticality of form itself is a strong characteristic of most of these objects and as such is conducive to horizontal banding.

It is not uncommon to derive pleasure from the beauty of nature, nor is it uncommon to want to convey those pleasures to the home. The vase assists us in this desire. The beauty of this art form, however, lies not only in its utility but in the beauty imparted in the pot by the potter as well.

The vase acts as the foundation for the everyday admiration and appreciation for that even greater and magnificent beauty offered to us freely by nature herself.

[1] Yanagi, Soetsu, *The Unknown Craftsman*, p. 155.

[2] Hopper, Robin, *Functional Pottery: Form and Aesthetic of Pots of Purpose*, p. 180.

Put A Lid On It

*H*and craftsmanship, if it be alive, justifies itself at any time as an intimate expression of the spirit of man. Such work is an end in itself and not a means to an end. If however, it ceases to serve a functional need, it runs the risk of becoming art for art's sake and untrue to its nature, depending upon the sincerity of the craftsman.[1]

Bernard Leach

A covered jar can never be art for art's sake. Its form is defined by the idea of a closed yet accessible useful volume. Anyone who has made a ceramic covered jar and has accidentally fused a lid to the form can appreciate the frustration and disappointment in the loss of this most salient and valued feature.

Clasped in an intimate embrace, the covered jar sequesters its secrets quite naturally. This ceramic form gently but dutifully impedes unwanted entry yet allows access when required.

Opposite in character to plates, platters and trays, covered jars and other lidded ceramic forms have sculptural attributes distinctly their own. Quintessentially, these pots define space and volume, and the usefulness of these defined spaces speaks volumes for the versatility of this particular pottery form. Furthermore, the creative delineation of the all-encompassing clay skin speaks volumes to the imagination of the artist.

"Clay offers itself to me as my partner in creating and discovering. It continues to move with me and draws me into its endless promises, victories and disappointments."
Ardis A. Bourland

"Moon Box," stoneware, 5" x .25" x 3.25", thrown and altered, soda/salt fired, C. 10. Photo by Fareed Al-Mashat.

"My intent is to surprise the viewer by defining the function of the vessel through the image and the setting the piece is placed in."
Kathy King

"Pregnancy Test Container," porcelain, 6.5" x 7" x 3.5", carved porcelain, C. 6. Photo by artist.

Moreover, the lidded ceramic container finds ample employment for the storage of a diverse range of objects in addition to food. The idea of containment of particular items may motivate the potter towards unique creative solutions.

Any material requiring protection from contamination or marauders may find safe refuge inside a ceramic container. Historically, foods of all types were the most likely candidates to be protected and stored. As a result, potters have produced numerous types of covered jars, canisters, and lidded forms that directly cater to the diverse needs and requirements of the dining room, kitchen, pantry, or cupboard.

And each type of storable material influences the qualities the potter may incorporate into the ceramic form. For example, special substances like sugar, spices or other condiments may inspire the potter in the direction of analogous, small scale ceramic forms.

On the other hand, containers intended for plentiful, bulky or staple items suggest a concurrent increase in scale, volume and practicality. As a result, these particular forms may reflect a more straightforward sturdiness that is more yeoman-like in character.

As with other ceramic forms, the selection of the particular clay body dramatically influences the expressive character and functionality of a covered jar. Earthenware clays, for example, are eminently appropriate for baking purposes and oven use. The porosity of earthenware contributes to its ability to withstand the thermal stresses associated with baking. Fortunately, the oven's gradual rise and fall in temperature permits the use of many different clays.

"I have chosen to make functional pots because I feel it helps me connect with people on a very basic human level."
Sandi Pierantozzi

"Spice Jar Set," earthenware, 6" x 16" x 6", slab built, C. 04-05. Photo by artist.

"The challenge of working within the parameters of utility while seeking forms and surfaces that are stimulating to our senses is the driving force behind my creative efforts."

Charity Davis-Woodard

"Longhouse Box," porcelain, 4" x 10" x 4", slip, glazes, forged steel, nichrome wire, C. 10. Photo by Jeffrey Bruce.

However, more densely fired clay bodies, like porcelain and stoneware, while fully capable of being for this purpose, are less resistant to thermal shock than their lower fired cousins.

Heat shock, produced by direct contact with a flame, will crack most pots no matter what type of clay is used. Special clays have been formulated for this practice. However, few potters use these clays since significant glaze fit problems are presented and the working qualities of the plastic clay are generally poor. As a result, pots made from this type of "flame-proof" clay are not commonly available.

But ceramic cooking casseroles are, indeed, designed to be used. Accessibility, ease of handling

"I think of functional pots as the most intimate of art forms. Every time I use a pot of someone's, I feel an instant link to that person."

Linda McFarland

"Altered Casserole," stoneware, 5.5" x 8" x 6", thrown, stretched, darted, salt fired, C. 10. Photo by Tom Mills.

"The accessibility of the handmade object in today's world seems vital and radical, and hopefully tempers our hunger for 'progress' and rationality."

Michael Kline

"Triphid Jar," stoneware, 12" x 12" x 10", thrown and altered, under glaze, wood fired with salt, C. 10. Photo by Walker Montgomery.

"My current work attempts to synthesize the casual and spontaneous traditions of folk pottery with a modernist and contemporary design sensibility."

Alex Karros

"Cheese Bell," porcelain, 13" x 9", wheel thrown with glazes, C. 6. Photo by John Woodin.

"My own work is informed by looking at daily life as subject matter for patterns for my pottery."

Richard Hensley

"Jewelry Box," porcelain, 4" x 5" diameter, wheel thrown and hand painted, C. 10. Photo by Tim Barnwell.

and cleaning are essential components of this kind of pot. Since they are often grasped while hot, these items need proportionally larger handles that can be understood by mitten-clad hands. All in all, these pots are designed to take the heat while performing useful service.

Notwithstanding utilitarian considerations, the relationship between the lid and the body of any covered jar does much to establish the expressive orientation of the pot. Normally, the slightly arched plate-like ceramic lid spans a deeper, wider volume. This is the typical arrangement for this helmeted

"Art is about communication."

Sandy Simon

"Sailor," porcelain, 5" x 5" x 5", thrown with nichrome wire, C. 8. Photo by Joe Schopplein.

ceramic armada. But this is by no means the only formal possibility.

Butter dishes and cheese bells have the opposite orientation in terms of their three-dimensional qualities. In these forms the proportions between the body and lid reverse themselves. The voluminous hanger-like lid acts as the benevolent protector of the languorous substance within. Innumerable variations in the proportions between lid and body are possible and they may often take their cues from the nature of the material to be stored.

This meeting place can also be subtly handled to emphasize the overall form in contrast to the distinct character that often exists between lid and body.

Technically, the potter needs to accent a healthy relationship between the lid and body of the covered jar. The connection point between the two forms is a critical juncture. The type of interaction between the two essential ceramic elements at this line often centers the expressive character of the pot.

For example, the lid of the container may rest upon an inside rim or gallery of the form and describe a more unified overall three-dimensional shape. The outside contour line of the pot being uninterrupted, will promote a more stoic or reserved quality to the form. It is as if the containment of the interior space has become the preeminent focal point of expressive energy of the form.

On the other hand, the lid designed to overhang the main body of the form is considerably more energetic sculpturally. These types of lids have

"My functional pots add another dimension, I hope, to the user's everyday life."

Mathew Metz

"Jar," porcelain, 9" high, thrown, wood/oil/salt fired, C. 10. Photo by Peter Lee.

"I think the truth is the ceramic medium does not translate to the written word."

Wayne Branum

"Covered Jar," stoneware, 11" high, hand built, wood and salt fired, C. 9-10. Photo by Peter Lee.

"I find inspiration in surfaces of all kinds, eroded steel, peeling paint, rocks and geological forms."

Jay Jensen

"Jar," stoneware, 10" x 14" x 6", thrown and hand built, soda fired, C. 10. Photo by Peter Lee.

"I am very concerned about the quality of workmanship, the color and texture of the glazes and the balance and feeling of each piece."

Janet Buskirk

"Covered Jar," white stoneware, 10" x 7" x 7", wheel thrown and combed, C. 10. Photo by Bill Bachhuber.

"It is my intent to assimilate many influences, combining them with a personal artistic perspective to design and produce unique, well-conceived, individual functional ware."
David Crane

"Green Box," stoneware, 9" x 6", thrown and altered, salt glazed, C. 10. Photo by Tim Barnwell.

"My interest is functional pottery meant to compliment domestic life."
Linda Arbuckle

"Biscuit Jar: Tall, Hot," terracotta, 8" x 12", wheel thrown, majolica glaze, C. 04. Photo by artist.

a cantilevered feel to them that is more inclined to emphasize the exterior space of the covered jar. Acting as an eave, this type of lid has more architectural implications.

Architecture, with its useful interior volumes and dynamic exterior articulations, is a fitting analogous art form when considering ceramic covered jars. Potters are aware of this and as a result visual references to buildings in covered jar forms are not uncommon.

Cap lids, drop-in lids that rest on a flange, flush lids, or lids cut directly from a completely closed form have their own distinctive part to play in the overall character of the form. Conical, strongly curved or spherical lids can suggest an organic fecundity that is ripe with emotional and expressive associations. In contrast, drop-in lids will enhance the importance of the body of the form because the lid itself is obscured by the container.

The care taken by the potter in fitting the lid to the main body is also very important. Craftsmanship is a form of quality control and plays an essential role in the aesthetic performance of a pot. A lid that is just fractions too large can produce an unpleasant tightness that will also encourage chipping with use. On the other hand, a loose-fitting lid is careless in feeling and suggests inattention, or worse, lack of skill on the part of the potter. There should be an adequate sense of "ease" in the physical connection between the lid and body.

In addition, the fired density of the clay body influences the sound produced when these two elements meet. Some potters prefer clay bodies that produce a soft, muffled, chafing sound when lid and pot join. In contrast, a very dense, tight, glassy body will produce a hard, flinty sound that some may consider unpleasant. It is in the practice of using handmade pottery that these subtleties and nuances may be discerned.

Since covered jars can fulfill so many purposes, they can vary dramatically in scale. Small covered pots are easily picked up and held. Their small diameter makes for eminently graspable lids. Consequently, knobs or handles are superfluous since the span of the fingertips is sufficient to separate the forms.

And as the scale of covered jars increases, so then does the need and desire to add knobs, finials, handles or lugs to assist handling.

These added elements have obvious practical implications but they also will be points of sculptural interest. Items that produce visual echoes to the

"There's something very tangible to me about producing things that are destined for the kitchen or dining room...enriching the day-to-day experience of living beyond the kind of influence that sculpture or a painting can transmit through the eyes."

Lisa Naples

"Soup Tureen," earthenware, 12" x 15" x 15", slab built, slips, glaze, C. 04. Photo by James Quale.

main body of the shape help to unify the form, while counter-intuitive additions can provide dynamic interest and fascinating contrasts. Many potters take particular joy in the creation of interesting knobs, handles and lugs that add specific unique visual/spatial characteristics to pots while simultaneously improving their utilitarian prospects.

Clary Illian emphasizes this idea when she instructs beginning potters by saying, "Make as many pulled, rolled, squeezed, cut, and constructed handles as you can bear to make. The more playful your approach, the more success you will have. Think of them as little sculptures."[2]

The message sent by a handle pulled directly from the clay is distinctly different than a handle that has been carved from a leather hard block of clay. Overall, the aesthetic response depends upon how the individual elements interact with one another.

The proportional relationships among all of the parts of the pot have important expressive implications, and this is particularly true of the covered jar. Whether it be a cheese bell, cookie jar, tea caddy, butter dish, casserole, storage jar or any other kind of container, the constituent parts of these useful items exist because potters enjoy solving a practical problems in an artful and expressive way.

The best covered jars are those that succeed simultaneously as works of art and as practical, efficient tools for living. As Robin Hopper has so succinctly stated, "Making good pottery is not making art for art's sake, it is making art for people's sake."[3]

---

[1] Yanagi, Soetsu, *The Unknown Craftsman*, p. 97.

[2] Clay Illian, *A Potter's Workbook*, p. 72.

[3] Hopper, Robin, *Functional Pottery*, p. 152.

Pour It On

Originally the hand craftsman was a supplier of all man's basic needs. He can never be that again. Today he is more and more both the rival and the ally of the fine artist.[1]

Edward Lucie-Smith

Without proper forms to shape the flow of liquids, life would be quite the messy affair. For liquids of all types, pouring vessels incorporate within their design the necessary elements for containment, hydraulic control and direction. The variations of body, spout, handle or lid found in these kinds of forms are limitless, yet each vessel must perform its function efficiently and uniquely without embarrassing either its owner or maker.

Pitchers, ewers, cruets, coffeepots (covered or not), jugs, spouted bowls or bottles, sauce boats, and teapots make up, for the most part, the pottery forms that are designed to spill liquids in a civilized fashion. These types of pouring vessels exist at the critical nexus of both utility and expressive form.

Like their ceramic brethren, these pots

"Teapots are a potter's challenge. It is a challenge to unify the many parts of the form and to design a surface decoration that compliments that form."
Marilyn Dennis Palsha

"Blue Swirl Teapot," earthenware, thrown and altered, majolica glazed, C. 03. Photo by Seth Tice Lewis.

"For me, the ceramic form often becomes a three-dimensional canvas on which to express my gestural ideas."
Kathy Erteman

"Teapot," whiteware, 6" x 6", wheel thrown, carved, C. 2. Photo by D. James Dee.

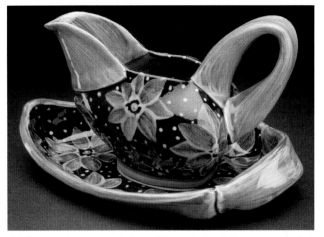

"Utility matters to me. It doesn't have to be at the expense of beauty, but the apparent beauty must not inhibit the intended use."
Lisa Naples

"Sauce Boat," earthenware, 5" x 9" x 6.5", slab built, slips, glaze, C. 04. Photo by James Quale.

"I want my pottery to be of service, soulful and spirit-filled."
Terry Gess

"Teapot," stoneware, 8" high, thrown and hand built, salt glazed, C. 10. Photo by Tim Barnwell.

"My intent is to make useful pots that function well and at the same time offer an aesthetic alternative to some familiar objects."
Charity Davis-Woodard

"Cordovan Teapot," red earthenware, 7" x 11.5" x 5.5", thrown and altered, hand-built components, terra sigillata, glaze, oxide wash, C. 04. Photo by David Kingsbury.

may manifest a profuse variety of unique shapes. Distinctively appealing sculptural forms combined with a specific, practical function are entwined. The spout, handle, body and lid of these forms must cooperate in a sophisticated and complex alliance of visual, spatial, surface and tactile relationships for the pot to succeed.

And, as is the case with many other pots, these forms are destined for the table and dining experiences.

There are an infinite number of ways of interpreting particular pottery forms. Some teapots may be created primarily as an exercise in the exploration of sculptural form. As a result, they may rarely be used since the constituent elements, interesting though they may be, are ill conceived for practical purposes.

Without doubt some non-utilitarian teapots succeed aesthetically just as some utilitarian teapots fail on visual/tactile grounds. Pouring vessels can have numerous and unique incarnations, each being more interesting or curious than the next. But the best vessels handle and pour as beautifully as they look. Spouts flair pleasingly in a visual way and simultaneously direct the flow of the liquid in an efficient and useful manner. Handles loop gracefully or emphatically while providing sufficient space for the secure grasp and balance of the pitcher. Teapot spouts taper or elongate in such a way as to add peculiar and provocative visual energy to the form while directing a spirited flow of brew to the cup.

In this balance between beauty and use the potter adds joy to life. It is this equilibrium that is sought in the attempt to capture a moment's significance in something as common as a syrup pitcher or a cream and sugar set.

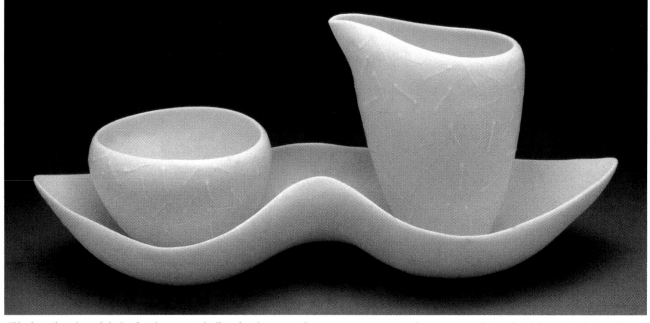

"My functional work is by far the most challenging because there are so many requirements predetermined for each design."
Elizabeth Lurie

"Creamer & Sugar Set with Tray," porcelain, 11" x 7" x 4", thrown and altered, hump molded, C. 9.5. Photo by Neil Lurie.

To be successful, all pottery must succeed as a utilitarian, three-dimensional art object. That is, the best pots are those that have uniquely engaging positive and negative form relationships or whose overall three-dimensional character is conspicuously strong and reflects an individual's unique artistic sensibility.

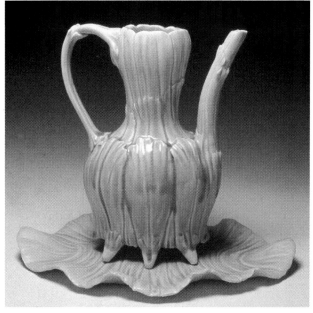

"I hope to show the beauty that can be found in nature and, in doing so, wish to make the viewer more aware of the life around them."
Bonnie Seeman

"Ewer & Tray," porcelain, 10" x 7" x 8", wheel thrown and altered, C. 10. Photo by artist.

As Wayne Higby, professor of ceramics at Alfred University states, "Functional pottery puts many restrictions on expression. It takes a highly sensitive, inventive and patient individual to turn these constraints into pottery. The teapot must pour. It must be well balanced at a comfortable scale. Its handle must provide security in lifting and its lid shouldn't fall into the cup as the tea flows from the spout."[2]

The teapot form, in particular, is noteworthy since it is certainly the most difficult exemplar of the potter's challenge to balance and harmonize both expressive and utilitarian values. The aesthetic resolution of the individual forms that comprise the teapot must occur in a harmonic or unified fashion.

To say the least, the teapot or pitcher form is an immensely formidable and complex form for the artist to explore. But for some potters there are still further challenges.

For example, one of the more interesting recent developments in contemporary American pottery is the exploration of ensemble sets of ceramic objects. These are suites of pots that are directly related to each other by virtue of their practical purpose and the physical characteristics they share.

The tea service, with its creamer, sugar jar, serving tray and extensive history, is but one example of this type of work. But other combinations of forms are available for manipulation and creative exploration as well.

This multiple object challenge is formidable since the positive and negative aspects of the assem-

"In making cream and sugar sets I am most curious about their own inherent dialogue; the set itself is reminiscent of close conversations."
Julia Galloway

"Cream & Sugar Set," porcelain, 3" x 2" x 3", thrown and hand built, soda fired, gold luster, C. 6. Photo by artist.

bled forms are richer and much more complex. Similar to the issues presented to the two dimensional still-life painter, these suites of objects become an actual three-dimensionalized still-life problem for the potter. While all of the aesthetic challenges such color, pattern, texture, value, hue, shape, and composition that face the painter are present, the potter is further required to actually create the objects themselves.

But these ceramic creations are no mere props for aesthetic research since these works of art can be used everyday.

This ceramic "still life" is no longer still since the owner or user of the pottery suite has the option of recombining or rearranging these formations as the situation or context suggests. These compositions, unlike their painted still life cousins, can be reconfigured at the discretion of the owner. In this sense the imaginative playfulness found to

be part and parcel of the original creation continues long after the pots have left the potter's studio.

Cruet sets, oil and vinegar sets, and the standard teapot service with its attendant drinking cups and serving tray all partake of the ensemble approach to pottery making.

The kinds of forms the potter elects to explore are unlimited as long as the potter has the requisite skills to produce them. The exceptional artist can imagine any unique shape as the basis for a teapot or pouring vessel and, with the appropriate technical means, produce them.

Obviously, the more complex and articulated the three-dimensional form the more those elements garner the attention of the viewer/user. The exploitation of contrasts in regard to texture, value, color, shape and pattern are essential in the production dynamic expression. The balance between complexity of shape and resolution of surface

"I truly believe that a handmade pot contains the soul and energy of the person who made it, and that a real human connection is made whenever someone uses it."
Sandi Pierantozzi

"Cream & Sugar Set," earthenware, 5" x 9" x 5", slab built, C. 04-05. Photo by artist.

"I am keenly interested in the unpredictability of the firing process and exploring how flame, ash, and volatile fluxes create a surface that is dictated by their passage over the form."
Thomas Rohr

"Autumn," porcelain, 16" x16", thrown, wood fired, C. 12. Photo by artist.

"I'm drawn to the beauty and mystery of high-temperature melting and the element of chance that occurs in atmospheric firings."
Josh DeWeese

"Liquor Set," porcelain, 10" x 13" x 10", wheel thrown, soda fired, C. 10. Photo by artist.

"The arrangement of related forms, like a still life, sets up relationships, and suggests the event (breakfast) at which these characters might be players."
Friederike Rahn

"Gourd Form Pitcher," earthenware, 10" x 7" x 5", thrown and hand built, terra sigillata, glazes, C. 04. Photo by artist.

enhancements needs also to be taken into account by the artist.

On the other hand, it is interesting to note how straightforward and uncomplicated some forms may be while still able to articulate the unique aesthetic concerns of their makers. This is so because the aesthetic power of the object lies not just in the three-dimensional aspects of the form, but in the way the artist has handled surface characteristics or pictorial imagery presented there. Relatively simple cones, cylinders, and spheres, or their varied segmented combinations, can be the platform from which other more engaging aesthetic surface elements may be played out.

Historically, ceramic vessels designed to pour liquids have been an integral part of people's lives in many cultures and societies for many centuries. For example, before the advent of indoor plumbing and running water, the ceramic pitcher and basin were standard features of the home.

Today, this venerable ceramic pitcher is not nearly as ubiquitous as in the past but it is still required to transfer liquids from one place to another. With ready-made, disposable plastic or cardboard utensils, most people today appear content with mass-produced items to fulfill these basic functions. It is the explosion in the use and availability of disposable products that has lessened the necessity of pottery in general and the pouring vessel in particular.

"A pot that captures my attention over time is not unlike a favorite book, revealing new layers of meaning with each reading."
Linda Christianson

"Cooking Oil Cans," stoneware, 8" x 7" x 7", thrown and hand built, wire and clay handle, wood fired, C. 10. Photo by artist.

On the other hand, since these mass-produced, negligibly significant items have replaced the omnipresent handmade ceramic items of the past, the craft person's individually created forms naturally become more significant and valuable.

What makes these forms and activities special and powerful are the significant and meaningful references that are made by the artist with these forms. The elements of the human figure and animal forms can be embodied in pouring vessels like pitchers or teapots.

The teapot is one of the most anthropomorphic of all pottery types. That is, with asymmetrical stance, jutting handle and curvaceous forms, the pitcher reminds us of the human body or perhaps some other creature.

The spout of the teapot appears to have undeniable phallic implications that can be more or less obvious. And some artists exploit this characteristic as a fundamental element of their expressions.

There are other nuanced suggestions of body language in the handle of pouring vessels. The handle of the teapot arches away from the body of the

"I have an interest in the tortoise-shell shape simply as a beautiful natural form and its ability to introduce animated qualities into functional pottery forms."
Sam Chung

"Tortoise Teapot," porcelain, 5" x 7" x 3", hand built and thrown, soda fired, C. 10. Photo by artist.

"I place my formal concerns first—while being ever mindful of the need for reasonable function in an object such as a pitcher or teapot."
Joseph D. Van Zandt

"Soy Cruet," stoneware, 6" x 6", thrown and altered, C. 9. Photo by artist.

"The familiar becomes abstracted."
Mark Pharis

"Yellow Teapot," earthenware, 9.5" x 9" x 6.5", hand built, C. 04. Photo by Peter Lee.

"My work is driven by the desire to discover and express the essence of that which is common or everyday."
Jessica L. Dubin

"Pitcher," stoneware, 12" x 6" x 4", thrown, pulled handle, wood fired, C. 10. Photo by Howard Goodman.

teapot in the fashion of the hand of a person resting on the hip. Some artists boldly accentuate these references to the human body in their pottery, while subtle affinities to the figure are veiled visual suggestions in the work of other potters.

Innumerable subjects from nature, whether they be animal, vegetable or mineral, have been transformed by potters into pouring vessels that have their own unique character.

For example, some studio potters are inspired by animal subjects. Elephants whose trunks literally act as water spouts are likely candidates for sculptural interpretations in teapot form. And these forms can be exceptionally successful both as sculptural form and utilitarian teapot. But it is the appropriateness of the trunk form in its utilitarian role as a teapot's spout that inspires the compelling conception in the first place.

Whether directly or indirectly related to the human figure, whether abstract or representational, pouring vessels can be very simple and straightforward in terms of their sculptural form or they may be exceptionally complex. But the overall impact they may have is one that is based in the performance of life-affirming activities that are enjoyed and appreciated day in and day out.

As critic and ceramics gallery director Garth Clark has noted, "Indeed the long love affair with this modestly scaled, spouted vessel shows no sign of abating. Our enduring fascination with the form grows from the intriguing interplay of familiarity and complexity. But the teapot also evokes deeply sensual feelings and memories. It resonates with the misty warmth of family gatherings redolent with fragrances not just of tea but of glowing fireplaces, freshly baked scones, and damp afternoons."[3]

Pots that pour are simply beautiful tools that offer a dense matrix of pleasurable feelings that enrich and make special the everyday tasks of life. Today's potters still produce wonderful, varied, exciting and beautiful work. For this, the rest of us can be extremely thankful.

[1] Lucie-Smith, *The Story of Craft: The Craftsman's Role in Society*, p. 8.

[2] Higby, Wayne, "Useful Pottery", *Ceramics Monthly*, p. 51.

[3] Clark, Garth, *The Eccentric Teapot*, p. 63.

Afterword

We currently face an enormous quantity of provocative and decidedly anti-utilitarian art made in craft media. At a time when so much work can be produced, get displayed in top-dollar real-estate venues, command high prices, become the subject of academic discourse, and function as a signifier of class and sophistication, it is especially pressing to continue making and appreciating handmade useful pots. Their value remains and asserting that value remains imperative. Wit, cleverness, commentary and technical virtuosity serve their social functions but we are still thirsty.

In using pottery we find affirmation of the sense of touch. The physical imprint of the potter's hands on wet clay is evident in every fired fingerprint and throwing line. The anthropomorphic and zoomorphic qualities of pots are humorously spelled out for us here as we are invited to imagine plates as stable soldiers of service and other pots as workhorses or ballet dancers. Through use these pots are animated. They move and gesture as if alive. And it is this physical interaction and closeness that makes the best case for use. When hand grips handle and lip touches cup's lip we know more completely what we hold. The hand must educate the mind. How infrequently is this demanded of us? Yet how essential the dictate. So much of what is asked of us relies on the senses of sight: The dashboard, the computer monitor, the television, the logo. How desperately do we need to reacquaint ourselves with touch? Every pot carries its message of heat and heft, of sandy or smooth, of its capacity. Every pot instructs us in tactile detail even without our conscious consideration.

How frequently on picking up a pot for the first time have I felt the inner exclamation "oh no, this is not what I thought!" as all the assumptions based on visual cues crumble with the first physical contact with the pot. New students have remarked how strange, even intrusive, it seemed at first to ask questions concerning form and to get the response "let's see" with both hands reaching for the pot. I've been teased by the eyes in my hands more than once. We need touch to help us set the record straight on all we incorrectly assume based on sight. Touch is the shortcut to accurately evaluating the balanced form. Touch provides information and pleasure we will find no other way.

In *"The Art of Contemporary American Pottery,"* use is addressed—its relevance to contemporary pottery and its function in building our understanding and appreciation. Now for beauty. To take up the subject of beauty while discussing any area of contemporary art takes a great deal of courage. It isn't fashionable, it isn't hip, it is rarely even considered an avenue of conversation relevant to art made in our time. But these nineteen chapters affirm the necessity of beauty. The illustrations and quotations from potters and writers have been marshaled to bolster the assertion that the experience of beauty is worthy of pursuit. The experience of beauty can be for every day, for every meal, at every table. It can be experienced at home without travel or tremendous expense. This is remarkable. This is worthy of celebration. This is very good news.

But there is work still to do. Through this book we have been given a charge. We makers and appreciators of pots are challenged to demand beauty, to expect it, to search it out, to create it, and to enjoy it.

—Louise Harter

"Figured Teapot,"
Kevin A. Hluch,
porcelain, 5.5" x 9" x 10",
hand built, C. 6.
Photo by Dan Meyers.
Collection of the author.

Appendix A
Addresses of Selected Potters

While many of the potters illustrated in this book exhibit and sell their works in galleries (see Appendix B) their work can also be acquired by visiting the potters themselves. Some potters are available for studio/gallery visits by appointment (*) while others have predetermined gallery hours (†). It is advisable to call the individual artist to enquire about forthcoming exhibitions, fairs, festivals, open houses or kiln openings or to ask that your name be added to their particular invitation mailing list.

*Stanley Mace Andersen
187 Water St.
Bakersville, NC 28705
Home   (828) 688-2645
E-mail kbasen@m-y.net

*Linda Arbuckle
14716 SE 9th Terrace
Micanopy, FL 32667
Home   (352) 466-3520
Fax   (352) 466-4965
E-mail arbuck@ufl.edu

* †Christa Assad
5 Sonoma St., Apt. #3
San Francisco, CA 94133
Home   (415) 788-0967
        (415) 440-2898
E-mail christaassad@hotmail.com
http://christaassad.8m.com

*Posey Bacopoulos
40 Fifth Ave. #14D
New York, NY 10011-8843
Work   (212) 431-7631
Home   (212) 533-9688
E-mail Poseyb@aol.com
http://www.silverhawk5.com/bacopoulos/index.html

Rob Barnard
597 South Middle Road
Timberville, VA 22853
Home   (540) 896-2769
E-mail Rbarnard@cfw.com

Bruce Barry
337 Adams St., P.O. Box 117
Milton, MA 02186
Home   (617) 696-4680
www.brucebarry.com

*D.Hayne Bayless
56 A Pond Meadow Road
Ivoryton, CT 06442
Home   (860) 767-3141
E-mail sideways@snet.net
www.sidewaysstudio.com

*†Susan Beecher
2070 Route 23C
East Jewett, NY 12424
Studio   (212) 749-4756
Home   (518) 589-6225

*†Joseph Bennion
Horseshoe Mountain Pottery
278 South Main St., P.O. Box 186
Spring City, UT 84662
Home   (435) 462-2708
E-mail joe.the.potter@rocketmail.com

*Jill Bonovitz
919-21 South 7th St.
Philadelphia, PA 19147
Studio   (215) 465-3364
E-mail Dmh03@earthlink.net

Ardis Bourland
1433 Mantua Ave.
Coral Gables, FL 33146
Home   (305) 661-4371
E-mail Sidra@mindspring.com

*Wayne Branum
610 North Third St.
Stillwater, MN 55082
Home   (651) 439-6100
Fax   (651) 351-7327
        (715) 425-7910
E-mail wbranum@salaarc.com

*Robert Briscoe
2785 Stark Road
Harris, MN 55032
Home   (651) 674-4656
E-mail rbstonwr@ecenet.com

*†William Brouillard
1567 Lewis Dr.
Lakewood, OH 44107
Studio   (216) 566-7926
Home   (216) 696-6010
E-mail Wbrouillard@ameritech.net
Fax   (216) 228-2186

*Joan Bruneau
52W. 11th Ave.
Vancouver, B.C V5Y 1S5 Canada
Work   (604) 844-3801
Home   (604) 872-4115
E-mail Jbruneau@eciad.bc.ca

Donn Lloyd Buchfinck
1028 Montgomery St.
San Francisco, CA 94133
Home   (415) 399-0432
Pager   (415) 414-1608
E-mail claycincal@aol.com
ceramicsCA@Aol.com

*Janet Buskirk
3624 SE Yamhill St.
Portland, OR 97214
Home   (503) 231-2810
oregonpotters.org

*Victoria D. Christen
5708 N. Syracuse
Portland, OR 97203
Home   (503) 735-1783
E-mail vchristen@qwest.net

Connie Christensen
12482 W. Nevada Pl. #213
Lakewood, CO 80228
Home   (720) 963-8462
(303) 573-5903
E-mail Cchrist777@earthlink.net

*†Linda Christianson
35703 Vibo Trail
Lindstrom, MN 55045
Home   (651) 257-2374

Sam Chung
N. MI U., Dept. of Art & Design
Marquette, MI 49855
Home   (906) 226-7395
        (906) 227-1491
Fax   (906) 227-2276
E-mail schung@nmu.edu

*Sunyong Chung
800 Gullett St.
Austin, TX 78702
Fax   (512) 389-1920

*Bede Clarke
225 W. Sunnyridge Ln.
Columbia, MO 65202
Studio   (573) 443-0362
Home   (573) 882-7120
Fax   (573) 884-6807
E-mail Clarkerb@missouri.edu

Sam Clarkson
P.O. Box 6255
Snowmass, CO 81615
Fax   (970) 922-7432
Home   (814) 235-1534
E-mail Sclarksons@hotmail.com
sclarksons@hotmail.com

*†Robert Compton
2662 North 116 Road
Bristol, VT 05443
Home   (802) 453-3778
E-mail Robert@RobertComptonPottery.com
RobertComptonPottery.com

*David Crane
1449 Luster's Gate Road
Blacksburg, VA 24060
Home   (540) 961-2484
Work   (540) 231-5547
Fax   (540) 231-5761
E-mail dcrane@vt.edu
16 hands.com

*Kevin Crowe
1289 Falling Rock Dr.
Amherst, VA 24521
Home   (804) 263-4065
E-mail lcrowe@tnc.org

*†Val Cushing
R.R. 1, Box 236
1497 Water Wells Road
Alfred, NY 14803
Home   (607) 587-9193
Fax   (607) 587-9036
E-mail cushingve@infoblvd.net

*Larry Davidson
P.O. Box 858
Alto, NM 88312
Work   (505) 336-7739
E-mail larry@littlecreekpottery.com
http://littlecreekpottery.com

Malcolm Davis
2322 Nineteenth St., NW
Washington, DC 20009
Home   (202) 265-1819
        (304) 472-7043
E-mail SHINOM@aol.com

*Charity Davis-Woodard
5400 Melon Lane
Edwardsville, IL 65056
Home   (618) 692-6508
E-mail Cdwpotter@primary.net

Parker-Kuhns, Debbie & Karl
132 N. Main St.
Dolgeville, NY 13329
Home   (315) 429-8386
E-mail kkuhns@twcny.rr.com

†Josh DeWeese
2915 Country Club Ave.
Archie Bray Foundation
Helena, MT 59602
Home   (406) 443-4664
        (406) 443-3502
Fax   (406) 443-0934
E-mail josh@archiebray.org

*Meg Dickerson
9014 Fairview Road
Silver Spring, MD 20910
Home   (301) 585-9666
E-mail maddesign@earthlink.net

*Jessica Dubin
730 Hudson Ave.
Peerskill, NY 10566
Home   (914) 737-8066

*Eleanora Eden
Paradise Hill
Bellows Falls, VT 05101
Home   (802) 869-2003
E-mail Eden@sover.net
www.eleanoraeden.com

*†Randy Edmonson
Route 5, Box 1255
Farmville, VA 23901
Home   (804) 392-8069
E-mail Redmonso@longwood.lwc.edu

Sanam Emami
56 1/2 West University
Alfred, NY 14802
Home   (607) 587-9253
Studio   (607) 871-2458
E-mail sanamek@yahoo.com

Kathy Erteman
16 East 18th St.
New York, NY 10003
Home   (212) 929-3970
Fax   (212) 929-3527
E-mail Katzele@aol.com

*†Paul Eshelman
238 North Main St., P.O. Box 455
Elizabeth, IL 61028
Home   (815) 858-2568
        (815) 858-2327
E-mail eshelmanpottery@internetni.com
eshelmanpottery.net

†Stephen Fabrico
P.O. Box 27, 76 Church St.
Bloomington, NY 12411
Home   (845) 331-4760
Fax   (845) 338-1356
E-mail whitemud48@aol.com

*Anne Fallis-Elliott
434 Greenwich St.
New York, NY 10013
Home   (212) 966-7347
Fax   (212) 966-7347
E-mail FallisT@aol.com
www.azodnem./com/Lounge/Elliott.htm

*Susan Filley
51 Vincent Dr.
Mt. Pleasant, SC 29464
Home   (843) 971-9934
Fax   (843) 971-9105
E-mail SusanF@awod.com
susanf@awod.com

*†Dan Finnegan
106 Hanover St.
Fredricksburg, VA 22401
Home   (540) 371-7255
E-mail D.finnegan@att.com

*†Katherine Finnerty
85426 Ridgeway Rd.
Pleasant Hill, OR 97455
Home   (541) 744-0609

*Warren Frederick
7908 Cannonball Gate Road
Warrenton, VA 20186-9627
Home   (540) 347-3526
Fax   (540) 347-2939
E-mail wf@artistpotters.com
www.artistpotters.com

Julia Galloway
SAC Ceramics Dept.
RIT 73 Lomb Memorial Drive
Rochester, NY 14623
Home   (716) 529-3942
Fax   (716) 475-6447
E-mail juliagalloway@hotmail.com
www.rit.edu/CIAS/SAC

*†Willem Gebben
N8751 Cty. Road A
Colfax, WI 54730

Home   (715) 962-3660

†Terry Gess
P.O. Box 282
Penland, NC 28765
Home   (828) 688-3863
Fax   (828) 688-3863
E-mail tgess@main.mitchell.nc.us
terrygesspottery.com

*†John Glick
Plum Tree Pottery
30435 W. 10 Mile Rd.
Farmington Hills, MI 48336
Home   (248) 476-4875
Fax   (248) 615-7598
E-mail Glickptp@aol.com

*Steven Godfrey
Box 233992
Anchorage, AK 99523
Home   (907) 345-6519
          (907) 786-6920
E-mail afsmg@uaa.alaska.edu

*†DeBorah Goletz
1789 Macopin Road
West Milford, NJ 07480
Home   (973) 728-4889
Fax   (973) 728-4298
E-mail dgoletz@earthlink.net

*†Silvie Granatelli
407 Slusher Store Road
Floyd, VA 24091
Home   (540) 745-4613
E-mail stelli@swva.net

*Louise Harter
7 Carrington Rd.
Bethany, CT 06524
Home   (203) 393-9273
E-mail louiseharter@earthlink.net
www.home.earthlink.net/~louise harter

Rebecca Harvey
146 Hopkins Hall - 128 North Oval Mall
Columbus, OH 43210-1363
(614) 292-6058
Home   (614) 231-8137
Fax   (614) 292-1674
E-mail Harvey.113@osu.edu

Gwen Heffner
327 Chestnut St., Suite #3
Berea, KY 40403
Fax   (859) 986-1096
Home   (606) 723-7604
          (859) 986-1096

*Richard Hensley
1643 Starbuck Rd.
Floyd, VA 24091
Home   (540) 745-4624

*Jason Hess
910 Kirkman St.
Lake Charles, LA 70601
Home   (318) 494-5538
Work   (318) 475-5055
E-mail Jhess@laol.net

*Mark Hewitt
424 Johnny Burke Road
Pittsboro, NC 27312
Home   (919) 542-2371
Fax   (919) 542-6158
          (919) 542-2371
E-mail Hewitts@mindspring.com
          hewitts@mindspring.com

*†Steven Hill
Red Star Studios
821 West 17th St.
Kansas City, MO 64108
Studio   (816) 474-7316
Home   (816) 523-7316
E-mail Rstarhill@aol.com

Kevin A. Hluch
113 W. All Saints St.
Frederick, MD 21701
Home   301-662-0369
E-mail KAHluch@umd5.umd.edu
www.erols.com/mhluch/mudslinger.html

*Sheila Hoffman
3019 Macomb St., N.W.
Washington, DC 20008
Home   (202) 244-2410
E-mail Yurasheila@msn.com

*Clary Illian
1695 Dows St., Box 191
Ely, IA 52227
Home   (319) 848-4963

*Kate Inskeep
10992 Gold Hill Rd.
Boulder, CO 80302
Home   (303) 459-0511

*Sarah Jaeger
908 Broadway
Helena, MT 59601
Home   (406) 449-3786

*Jay Jensen
308 South Falls St.
River Falls, WI 54022
Home   (715) 425-2334
Fax   (715) 425-2334
E-mail jayjensn@pressenter.com
          www.mrpots.net

†Nicholas P. Joerling
P.O. Box 147
Penland, NC 28765
Home   (704) 765-5392

*Mark D. Johnson
83 Romano Road
South Portland, ME 04106
Home   (207) 767-7132
E-mail mjohnson@meca.edu

Shirley Johnson
262 Lake St.
Excelsior, MN 55331
Home   (612) 474-8616
E-mail shirleydoespots@aol.com

*Randy Johnston
N 8336 690th St.
River Falls, WI 54022
Home   (715) 425-5596
Fax   (715) 425-0657
E-mail Randy.johnston@uwrf.edu
http://www.uwrf.edu/rj16/?index.html

*†Fred Johnston
249 E. Main Street
Seagrove, NC 27341
Home   (336) 873-9380
Studio   (336) 873-9176
E-mail grolegg@asheboro.com

*†Alec Karros
317 Main Street, Mountainville
Lebanon, NJ 08833
Home   (908) 832-2932
E-mail bullseye@blast.net

Matt Kelleher
1641 Hauser Blvd.
Helena, MT 59601
Home   (406) 495-0064
E-mail Pothugger@aol.com
          Kelleher-Pottery.com

*Gail Kendall
3200 Van Dorn St.
Lincoln, NE 68502
Home   (402) 486-3775
Work   (402) 472-5548
Fax   (402) 472-9746
E-mail Gkendall@unl.edu

*Diane Kenney
0172 N. Bill Creek Road
Carbondale, CO 81623
Studio   (970) 963-2529
Home   (970) 963-2395
Fax   (970) 963-4492
E-mail Potter@aspeninfo.com

*Kristen Kieffer
2363 U.S. 33
Shade, OH 45776
Home   (740) 593-9725
kk248592@ohiou.edu

*Ashley Kim
1212 North Grant St. #B3
Bloomington, IN 47408
Studio   (812) 855-8738
Home   (812) 323-2659
E-mail Ashkim@indiana.edu

*Kathy King
904 Ponce de Leon Ave. NE, Apt. 1
Atlanta, GA 30306
Home   (404) 815-0051
Work   (404) 651-0587
E-mail kathykingklay@yahoo.com

*†Michael Kline
Penland Rd.
Penland, NC 28765
Home   (828) 688-9717
Studio   (828) 765-8583
Fax   (828) 765-7389
E-mail mkline@mitchell.main.us.nc

Maren Kloppmann
106 N. Sherburne St.
Stillwater, MN 55082
Home   (651) 351-7530
E-mail Marenk@earthlink.net

*Judy Kogod-Colwell
7325 Takoma Ave.
Takoma Park, MD 20912
Home   (301) 588-3634
Studio   (703) 548-0707
E-mail Judykogod@aol.com

*Ron Larsen
Crary Mills Pottery
174 County Route 35
Canton, NY 13617
Home   (315) 386-4721

*†Dick Lehman
1100 Chicago Ave.
Goshen, IN 46528
Work   (219) 534-2504
          (219) 534-1162
E-mail DickLehman@aol.com
www.DickLehman.com

*†Simon Levin
W 11561 Mill Creek Road
Gresham, WI 54128-9032
Home   (715) 787-4831
E-mail woodkiln@aol.com

*Robbie Lobell
145 Chaplin Street
Chaplin, CT 06235
Home   (860) 455-9522
E-mail marl@neca.com

*Cheri L. Long
Box 29, 1 Trinity Road
Marysville, MT 59640
Home   (406) 443-1427
E-mail cheripots@aol.com

*Jim Lorio
790 S. Cherryvale Road
Boulder, CO 80303-9707
Home   (303) 499-3850
E-mail MegjimLorio@earthlink.net

*Elizabeth Lurie
29228 Summerwood
Farmington Hills, MI 48334
Home   (248) 851-1732
E-mail nlurie@mich.com
www.artservemichigan.com/members/lurie

*†Warren MacKenzie
8695 68th St., N
Stillwater, MN 55082
Home   (651) 777-4979

*Peg Malloy
201 Stark Mesa Rd.
Carbondale, CO 81623-8914
Home   (970) 704-0862
E-mail Peg@sopris.net

*Polly Ann Martin
40 McEwen Street
Warwich, NY 10990
Home   (845) 987-1723
          (845) 986-9245
E-mail potters@warwick.net
          Fmartin@92NDSTY.org

*†Karen Thuesen Massaro
617 Arroyo Seco
Santa Cruz, CA 95060-3147
Home   (408) 429-5300
E-mail claypieces@hotmail.co
http://mambo.ucsc.edu/psl/km/karen.html

*Kate Maury
1725 Meadow Hill Drive
Menomonie, WI 54751
Home   (715) 235-6079

†Linda McFarling
Route 6, Box 246 Bolens Creek Road
Burnsville, NC 28714
Home   (828) 682-7150
Studio   (828) 682-7565
Fax   (828) 682-7550
E-mail Johnm@yancey.main.nc.us

*Jan McKeachie-Johnston
N 8336 690th St.
River Falls, WI 54022
Home   (715) 425-5596
Fax   (715) 425-0657
E-mail Rand.johnston@uwrf.edu
http://www.uwrf.edu/~rj16/index.html

*Alleghany Meadows
P.O. Box 781
Carbondale, CO 81623
Home   (970) 704-9901
E-mail Alleghany@hotmail.com

†Blair Meerfeld
555 8th St., P.O. Box 376 Hwy. 285
Saquache, CO 81149
Home   (719) 655-2682
E-mail mandmart@fone.net

*†Catherine Merrill
1456 Florida St.
San Francisco, CA 94110
Home   (415) 920-9390
E-mail CeramicsCA@aol.com

*†Valerie Metcalfe
796 Fleet Ave.
Winnepeg, MAnitoba R3M 1L4 Canada
Studio   (204) 475-8088
Home   (204) 475-6310
Fax   (204) 452-8212

*†Matthew Metz
P.O. Box 502
Alfred, NY 14802
Home   (507) 896-3068

Sequoia Miller
1019 Central St. SE
Olympia, WA 98501
Studio   (360) 357-6171
E-mail sequoia@olywa.net

*Steven Murphy
65 Chandler St.
Boston, MA 02116
Work   (617) 542-0997
www.bostonpottery.com

*Don Nakamura
627 N. 3rd St.
Philadelphia, PA 19123
Home   (215) 592-1581

*Lisa Naples
2321 Lower State Road
Doylestown, PA 18901
Home   (215) 340-0964
Fax   (215) 230-7652
E-mail pots@lisanaples.com
www.lisanaples.com

*†Dwain Naragon
510 E. Maple St.
Westfield, IL 62474
Home   (217) 967-5373
Studio   (217) 581-3410
E-mail Cfdln@eiu.edu

*†Dale Neese
11192 Baxtershire
San Antonio, TX 78254-1024
Home   (210) 688-9261
Fax   (210) 688-9145
E-mail d.neese@worldnet.att.net

Shannon Nelson
PO Box 61468
Fairbanks, AK 99706
Home   (907) 455-4356
E-mail clayfulcreations@yahoo.com

Katheleen Nez
P.O. Box 1561
Santa Fe, NM 87504
Home   (505) 992-0743
Fax   (505) 982-7171
E-mail www.knezbah@yahoo.com

Susan O'Brien
57 Rayburn Road
Murray, KY 42071
Fax   (270) 762-2588
Home   (270) 435-4460
E-mail susan.obrien@murraystate.edu

†Jeff Oestreich
36835 Pottery Trail
Taylors Falls, MN 55084

Home   (651) 583-2532

*Marilyn Palsha
45 Adna Pearce Road
Zebulon, NC 27597
Home   (919) 269-8760

Fax   (919) 269-4050

George Parker
324 Beckett Court
Winter Park, FL 32792

Home   (407) 679-2313

*Jess Parker
1700 La Vereda Road
Berkeley, CA 94709
Work   (415) 309-1409
Home   (415) 751-0380
E-mail jparkit@aol.com

Debra & Karl Parker-Kuhns
132 N. Main St.
Dolgeville, NY 13329

Home   (315) 429-8386

*Neil Paterson
2545 Meredith St.
Philadelphia, PA 19130

Home   (215) 763-8439

*Sara Patterson
19-21 23rd Dr.
Astoria, NY 11105
Home   (718) 267-2994

         (212) 873-8442

*Aysha Peltz
726 Townhill Rd.
Whitingham, VT 05361
Home   (802) 368-2807
Fax
E-mail Ayshapeltz@hotmail.com
www.ayshap.com

*Mark Pharis
1166 Coulee Trail
Roberts, WI 54023
Home   (715) 425-1597
Fax   (612) 625-7881
E-mail phari001@maroon.tc.umn.edu

*Sandi Pierantozzi
2545 Meredith St.
Philadelphia, PA 19103
Home   (215) 763-8439

*Pete Pinnell
2102 Lake St.
Lincoln, NE 68502
Home   (402) 435-2598
Studio (402) 472-4429
E-mail Ppinnell1@unl.edu

*Greg Pitts
433 Second St., # 3
Brooklyn, NY 11215
Studio (917) 837-4329
Home   (718) 768-5228
E-mail pittsg@mindspring.com

*†Sharon Pollock-De Luzio
151 Columbia Ave.
Cranston, RI 02905
Studio (401) 781-4439
Home   (401) 461-3528
E-mail Spollockdl@aol.com

*†Donna Polseno
1643 Starbuck Rd.
Floyd, VA 24091-4510
Home   (540) 745-4624
16hands.com

*Liz Quackenbush
268 Main St.
Pleasant Gap, PA 16823
Home   (814) 359-4327
Fax   (814) 359-4328
E-mail Lfq1@psu.edu

*Friederike Rahn
#305-1246 Cardero St.
Vancouver, B.C. V6A 2H2 Canada
Home   (604) 685-5176
Fax   (604) 254-3666
E-mail frahn85023@aol.com

*I.B. Remsen
214 Third St.
Ann Arbor, MI 48103
Home   (734) 996-0873
E-mail clayranger@aol.com
www.ibremsen-potter.com

*†Thomas Rhor
385426 Ridgway Road
Pleasant Hill, OR 97455
Home   (541) 744-0609

*Steven Roberts
317 1/2 Conneaut Ave.
Bowling Green, OH 43402
Home   (419) 352-4782
E-mail steven roberts@hotmail.com

*George Roby
92 E. Belmeadow Ln.
Chagrin Falls, OH 44022
Home   (440) 338-1777

*†Michael Roseberry & Bruce Winn
669 Elmwood Avenue
Providence, RI 02907
Home   (401) 941-3156
         (461) 941-8962
Fax   (461) 941-8962
E-mail roseberrywinn@mindspring.com
roseberrywinn.com

Will Ruggles & Douglass Rankin
736 Big Pine Way
Bakersville, NC 28705
E-mail pots@m-y.net
www.homestead.com/rockcreekpottery//index.html

*†James Sankowski
906 Saratoga Road
Ballston Lake, NY 12019
Home   (518) 399-1039

*Tom Schiller
3515 NE 48th Terr
Kansas City, MO 64119
Home   (816) 453-0708
E-mail Tmud58@hotmail.com

*Brad Schwieger
13350 Scatter Ridge Rd.
Athens, OH 45701
Home   (740) 593-3500

*†Ken Sedberry
344 Mine Creek Road
Bakersville, NC 28705
Home   (828) 688-3386
E-mail Sedberry@mitchell.main.nc.us
sedberrypottery.com

*Bonnie Seeman
9433 Chelsea Dr. South
Plantation, FL 33324
Fax   (305) 284-2115
Home   (954) 424-9441
         (305) 284-5470
E-mail BSSEE@aol.com
claysculpture.com

*Richard & Carol Selfridge
9844-88 Avenue
Edmonton, Alberta T6E2R3 Canda
Home   (780) 439-9296
Fax   (780) 434-9931
E-mail selfridg@compusmart.ab.ca
http://www.compusmart.ab.ca/selfridg

*Kate Shakeshaft Murray
1854 NW 41st Ave.
Gainesville, FL 32605
Home   (352) 337-9074
E-mail Roundear@mindspring.com
www.silverhawk5.com/murray

*†Ellen Shankin
297 Sumner Lane NE
Floyd, VA 24091
Home   (540) 745-3595
E-mail Warshank@swva.net
www.16hands.com

*†Linda Sikora
2 Pine St.
Alfred, NY 14802
E-mail sikoral@alfred.edu
Studio (607) 871-2461
Fax   (607) 871-2490

*Michael Simon
2270 Crawford Smithonia Road
Colbert, GA 30628
Home   (706) 788-3226

*†Sandra Simon
1306 Third St.
Berkeley, CA 94701
Home   (510) 526-3655
Fax   (510) 526-0279
E-mail Cone5@aol.com

*Willi Singleton
843 Hawk Mtn. Rd.
Kempton, PA 19529
Home   (610) 756-6387
E-mail Picrepot@voicenet.com
picrepot@voicenet.com

*Susan Sipos
4408 Dexter St.
Philadelphia, PA 19128
Fax   (215) 483-8707
Home   (215) 482-5681
E-mail Objectart@earthlink.net
         objectart@earthlink.net

*John Skelton
767 Blvd.
Macon, GA 31211
Home   (912) 746-1264
Fax
E-mail Skeltonjw@aol.com

*Lynn Smiser-Bowers
3715 Madison
Kansas City, MO 64111
Fax   (816) 753-8456
Home   (816) 561-1755
E-mail lbowers@ks.rr.com

*Gay Smith
1529 Cane Creek Road
Bakersville, NC 28705
Home   (828) 688-3686
E-mail ggspottey@aol.com

McKenzie Smith
C/O Horse Creek Pottery
6390 Anderson Way
Melbourne, FL 32940
Home   (321) 242-2162
E-mail kenziebs@hotmail.com

*†Michael Smith
1605 Locust
Kansas, MO 64108
Home   (816) 444-3590
Studio (816) 471-5466
E-mail mlspots@kc.net

*Ian Stainton
Box 105 A, RR 1
Spring Mills, PA 16875
Home   (814) 364-9974
E-mail shappite@aol.com

*Chris Staley
120 West Lytle
State College, PA 16801
Home   (814) 231-4890
         (814) 865-6412
E-mail Cxs41@psu.edu

*Lisa Stinson
129 Reklaw Drive
Bakersville, NC 28705
Home   (828) 688-4533
E-mail Stinsonlm@appstate.edu

*Richard Swanson
585 South Rodney
Helena, MT 59601
Home   (406) 442-8106
E-mail Richard@swanson.com
richard.swanson.com

Byron Temple
Post Box 7914
Louisville, KY 40257
Home   (502) 893-2684

*John Tilton
1611 NW 88th Terr.
Alachua, FL 32615
Home   (904) 462-3762
E-mail tilton@atlantic.net
www.tiltonpottery.com

Jack Troy
540 Shively Rd.
Huntington, PA 16652
Home   (814) 643-3554
E-mail jgaylordt@yahoo.com
         troy@juncol.juniata.edu

*Ann M. Tubbs
P.O. Box 208
Ottawa Lake, MI 49267
Home   (734) 856-1859
E-mail Abtubbs@glasscity.net

*†Bill Van Gilder
20834 Townsend Road
Gapland, MD 21779
Home   (301) 416-2970
Fax   (301) 416-2970
E-mail Vgpottery@hotmail.com

Joseph Van Zandt
14746 Shadeland Road
Springboro, PA 16435
Home   (814) 763-2001
E-mail joevanzandt@earthlink.net

Rimas VisGirda
317 Elmwood Drive
Champaign, IL 61821-3218
Home   (217) 398-1956
Studio (217) 359-4766
E-mail B-theide@uiuc.edu

*Todd Wahlstrom
726 Town Hill Rd.
Whitingham, VT 05361
Home   (802) 368-2807
E-mail Twah68@hotmail.com

Geoffrey Wheeler
221 1/2, 22nd Ave. E.
Menomonie, WI 54751
Home   (715) 235-7407
E-mail Wheelerg@uwstout.edu
E-mail Geoffreywheeler@hotmail.com
         wheelerg@uwstout.edu

*Catherine White
7908 Cannonball Gate Road
Warrenton, VA 20186-9627
         (540) 347-3526
Fax   (540) 347-2939
E-mail cw@artistpotters.com
www.artistpotters.com

*†Erica Wurtz
26 Parsons Road
Conway, MA 01341
Home   (413) 369-4006
E-mail ewbb@valinet.com
www.2studios.com

*Rosalie Wynkoop
2915 Country Club Ave.
Helena, MT 59601
Home   (406) 443-4664
         (406) 443-2969
E-mail rwynkoop@mcn.net

Appendix B
Galleries Representing Potters Selected for Book

Southern Highland Craft Guild
P.O. Box 9545
Milepost 382, Blue Ridge Parkway
Asheville, NC 28815
Work   (828) 298-7928
Fax   (828) 298-7962
www.southernhighlandguild.org

Carbondale Clay Center
135 Main St.
Carbondale, CO 81623
Work   (970) 963-2529

Earthworks Pottery
1705 First Ave. at 88 St.
NYC, NY 10128
Work   (212) 876-6945

Holter Museum of Art
12 East Lawrence St.
Helena, MT 59601
Work   (406) 441-6400
www.holtermuseum.org

Lill Street Gallery
1021 W. Lill St.
Chicago, IL 60614
Work   (773) 477-6185
Fax   (773) 477-5065
www.lillstreet.com

Pewabic Pottery
10125 E. Jefferson
Detroit, MI 48214
(313) 822-0954
www.pewabic.com

Vermont Clay Studio
2802 Waterbury-Stowe Rd. Route 100
Waterbury Center, VT 05677
Work   (802) 244-1126
http://www.vermontclaystudio.com/

Worcester Center for Crafts
25 Sagamore Rd.
Worcester, MA 01605
Other (508) 753-8138
http://www.craftcenter.worcester.org/

A Show of Hands Contemporary Craft Gallery
1016 Eglinton Ave. W.
Toronto, Ontario M6C 2C5 Canada
Work   (416) 782-1696
Fax   (416) 782-1890
www.ashowofhands.com

A' Mano
2707 Culver Road
Birmingham, AL 35223
Work   (205) 871-9093
Fax   (205) 871-1606

Akar A+D
4 S. Linn St.
Iowa City, IA 52240
Work   (319) 351-1227
Fax   (319) 887-2614

Alpha House Gallery
South St., Sherborne
Dorset   DT9 3LU United Kingdom
Work   44 (0) 01935-814944
Fax   44 (0) 1935-863932
alpha-house.co.uk

American Studio
2906 M. St. NW
Washington, D.C. 20007
Work   (202) 965-3273

Anderson Gallery
300 NE 3rd St.
McMinnville, OR 97128
Work   (503) 434-9292
Fax   (503) 434-1344
andersonartgallery.com

Ann Arbor Art Center
117 W. Liberty
Ann Arbor, MI 48104
Work   (734) 994-8004
Fax (734-994-3610
www.annarborartcenter.org

Annapolis Pottery
40 State Circle
Annapolis, MD 21401
Work   (410) 268-6153

Anton Gallery
2108 R. St. N.W.
Washington,   D.C. 20008
Work   (202) 328-0828
Fax   (202) 745-5842
www.antongallery.com

Appalachian Fireside Gallery
127 Main Street
P.O. Box 87
Berea, KY 40403
Work   (859) 986-9013

Appalachian Spring
102 W. Jefferson St.
Falls Church, VA 22046
Work   (703) 533-0930
Fax   (703) 533-1645

Archie Bray Foundation for the Ceramic Arts
2915 Country Club Ave.
Helena, MT 59602
(406) 443-3502
archiebray@archiebray.org
www.archiebray.org/

Ariana Gallery
119 S. Main
Royal Oak, MI 48067
Work   (248) 546-8810

Art Fusion
111 N. Higgins
Missoula, MT 59802
Work   (406) 549-3596

Artifacts Gallery
300 E. Main St.
Bozeman, MT 59715
Work   (406) 586-3755
Fax   (406) 586-2412

Artists On Santa Fe
747 Santa Fe Dr.
Denver, CO 80204
Work   (303) 573-5903

Ataz
3480 Galleria
Edina, MN 55435
Work   (612) 925-4883

Atlantic Beach Potters
400 Levy Road
Atlantic Beach, FL 32233
Work   (904) 249-4499

Avante Gallery
2062 Murray Hill Rd.
Cleveland, OH 44106
Work   (216) 791-1622
http://www.avantegallery.com/

Biddle Gallery
2840 Biddle Ave.
Wyandotte, MI 48192
Work   (734) 281-4779
www.biddlegallery.com

Blue Dome Gallery
307 N. Texas St.
Silver City, NM 88061
Work   (505) 534-8671
Fax   (505) 534-0822
www.zianet.com/bluedome

Blue Heron Gallery
Church St.
Deer Isle, ME 04627
Work   (207) 348-2940

Blue Spiral I
38 Biltmore Ave.
Asheville, NC 28801
Work   (828) 251-0202
Fax   (828) 251-0884
http://www.bluespiral1.com/

Bluestem Missouri Crafts
13 South Ninth St.
Columbia, MO 65201
Work   (573) 442-0211
Bluestemcrafts@earthlink.net

Boulder Arts & Craft Co-op
1421 Pearl St. Mall
Boulder, CO 80302
Work   (303) 443-3683

Branum/Pharis Studio
Fire No. 449, Valley View Road
Roberts, WI 54023
Work   (715) 425-7910

Brooke Pottery
213 East Bay St.
Lakeland, FL 33801
Work   (941) 688-6844
Fax   (941) 683-4759

Capital Gallery
314 Lewis St.
Frankfort, KY 40601
Work   (502) 223-2649
Fax   (502) 223-2975

Cedar Creek Gallery
1150 Fleming Rd.
Creedmoor, NC 27522
Work   (919) 528-1041
Fax   (919) 528-1120
http://www.cedarcreekgallery.com/

Center City Artisans
The Galleria
65 Neybosset St.
Providence, RI 02903
Work   (401) 521-2990

Center For Spirituality and the Arts
4707 Broadway
San Antonio, TX 78209
Work   (210) 829-5980

Clark Gallery
P.O. Box 339
Lincoln, MA 01773
Work   (781) 259-8303
Fax   (781) 259-8314
http://www.ClarkGallery.com/

Clay & Fiber Gallery
201 Paseo Del Pueblo Sur.
Taos, NM 87571
Work   (505) 758-8093
Fax   (505) 758-7179

Coda Gallery
73-151 El Paseo
Palm Desert, CA 92260-4225
Work   (800) 700-4661
Fax   (760) 776-4010

Concept Art Gallery
1031 S. Braddock Ave.
Pittsburgh, PA 15218
Work   (412) 242-9200

Contemporary Artifacts Gallery
327 Chestnut St. #3
Berea, KY 40403
Work   (859) 986-1096

Contemporary Crafts Gallery
3934 S.W. Corbett
Portland, OR 97201
Work   (503) 223-2654
Fax   (503) 223-0190

Craftspace Gallery
390 Academy Road
Winnipeg, Manitoba R3N 0B0
Work   (204) 487-6114
Fax   (204) 487-6115

Craftworks
Chalmers Building
35 McCaul St.
Toronto, Ontario M5T 1V7
Work   (416) 977-0891

Creative Works Gallery
80 Audubon St.
New Haven, CT 06510
Work   (203) 562-4927
Fax   (203) 562-2329

Dai Ichi Arts, Ltd.
24 W. 57th St., 6th Floor
New York, NY 10019
Work   (212) 262-0239
Fax   (212) 262-2330
www.daiichiarts.com

del Mano Gallery
11981 San Vincente Blvd.
Los Angeles, CA 90049
Work   (310) 476-8508

Departure Gallery
Albany International Airport, Suite 200
Albany, NY12211-1057
Work   (518) 242-2540
Fax   (518) 242-2544

Earth & Fire Gallery
775 Station St.
Herndon, VA 20170
Work   (703) 421-3887
Fax   (703) 421-4399

Earthworks
233 Haverford Ave.
Narbeth, PA 19072
Work   (610) 667-1143
Fax   (610) 667-1143

Elain Baker Gallery
608 Banyan Trail
Boca Raton, FL 33431
Work   (561) 241-3050
Fax   (561) 241-5976

Elliot Smith Contemporary Art
4727 McPhearson
St. Louis, MO 63108
Work   (314) 361-4800

Erl Originals
3069 Trenwest Drive
Winston-Salem, NC 27103
Work   (336) 760-4373
Fax   (360) 760-5953
www.erloriginals.com

Essentia
199 Boulston St.
Chestnut Hill
Boston, MA 02467
Work   (617) 244-4468

Eureka Crafts
210 Walton St.
Syracuse, NY 13202
Work   (315) 471-4601
eurekacrafts.com

Ferrin Gallery
163 Teatown Road
Croton On Hudson, NY 10520
Work   (914) 271-9362
Fax   (914) 271-0047
www.ferringallery.com

Fifth Element Gallery
404 NW 10th St., Suite 1
Portland, OR 97221
Work   (503) 279-9042

Figments
458 Ward St.
Nelson, B.C V1L 1S8
Work   (250) 354-4418

Fine Lines
304 S. Stratford Rd.
Winston-Salem, NC 27103
Work   (336) 723-8066

Finewares
7042 Carrol Ave.
Takoma Park , MD 20912
Work   (301) 270-3138

Fire Opal
320 Harvard St.
Brookline, MA 02446
Work   (617) 739-9066

Fisher Gallery Shop,
Farmington Valley Arts Center
25 Arts Center Lane
Avon, CT 06001
Work   (203) 678-1867

Florida Craftsmen Gallery
501 Central Ave.
St. Petersburg, FL 33701
Work   (813) 821-7391

Freehand
8413 W. 3rd St.
Los Angeles, CA 90048
Work   (323) 655-2607
Fax   (323) 655-7241

Fresh Pond Clay Works
368 Huron Ave.
Cambridge, MA 02138
Work   (617) 492-1907
Fax   (781) 648-8240

Gallery at Schenectady Museum
15 Nott Terrace Hgts.
Schenectady, NY 12308

Gallery Eight
7464 Girard Ave.
La Jolla, CA 92037
Work   (828) 454-9781
Fax   (828) 454-0804

Gallery Materia
4222 North Marshall Way
Scottsdale, AZ 85251
Work   (480) 949-1262
Fax   (480) 949-6050
www.gallerymateria.com

Gallery One
121 Scollard St.
Toronto, Ontario M5R 1GA
Work   (416) 929-3103
Fax   (416) 929-0278

Gallery Shop
818 Pike St.
Lemont, PA 16851
Work   (814) 234-2740

gallery WDO
Suite 610 @ Atherton Mill
2000 South Boulevard
Charlotte, NC 28203
Work   (704) 333-9123
Fax   (704) 376-9183
http://www.gallerywdo.com/

Garth Clark Gallery
24 West 57th St. No. 305
NYC, NY 10019
Work   (212) 246-2205
Fax   (212) 489-5168

Genovese/Sullivan
27 Thayer St.
Boston, MA 02118
Work   (617) 426-9738

Gifted Hand
32 Church St.
Wellesley, MA 02482
Work   (781) 235-7171

Graystone Gallery
3279 S.E. Hawthorne Blvd.
Portland, OR 97214
Work   (503) 238-0651

Hashimoto Bijutsu
3-come, 27-7 Sakae
Minami-otsu, Naka-Ku, Nagoya, Japan 302
Work   (052) 262-8470

Helen Drutt Gallery
1721 Walnut St.
Philadelphia, PA 19103
Work   (215) 735-1635

Hibberd McGrath Gallery
101 N. Main St.
P.O. Box 7638
Breckenridge, CO 80424
Work   (970) 453-6391

Hoadley Gallery
21 Church St.
Lenox, MA 01240
Work   (413) 637-2814
Fax   (413) 443-4713

Hoff Miller
595 S. Broadway #106E
Denver, CO 80209
Work   (303) 698-0800
Fax   (303) 722-9060

Illinois Artisans Shop
James R. Thompson Center
100 W. Randolph St., Suite 2-200
Chicago, IL 60601
Work   (312) 814-5321

Iowa Artisans Gallery
117 E. College St.
Iowa City, IA 52240
Work   (319) 351-8686
www.iowa-artisans-gallery.com/

Jean Wilson Gallery
233 Linden St.
Fort Collins, CO 80524
Work   (970) 407-1809

John Elder Gallery
529 W. 20th St.
New York, NY 10011
Work   (212) 462-2600
Fax   (212) 462-2510
www.johnelder.com

June Fitzpatrick Gallery
112 High St.
Portland, ME 04101
Work   (207) 772-1961

Kemper Museum of Contemporary Art Shop
4420 Warwick Blvd.
Kansas City, MO 64111
Fax   (816) 753-5806
http://www.kemperart.org/

Kentucky Art & Craft Gallery
609 W. Main St.
Louisville, KY 40202
Work   (502) 589-0102
Fax   (502) 589-0154
www.kentuckycrafts.net

Kobo Shop: Gallery
814 E. Roy St.
Seattle, WA 98102
Work   (206) 726-0704

Lacoste Gallery
25 Main St.
Concord, MA 01742
Work   (978) 369-0278
Fax   (978) 369-3375

Lincoln Art Pottery
636 W. Lincoln Ave.
Milwaukee, WI 53215
Work   (414) 643-1101
Fax   (414) 643-1158

Mackerel Sky Gallery
217 Ann St.
E. Lansing, MI 48823
Work   (517) 351-2211
Fax   (517) 351-5751

MacLaren/Markowitz
Pearl St.
Boulder, CO
Work   (303) 449-6807
Fax   (303) 444-6922

Macy Dorf/Artists On Santa Fe
747 Santa Fe Dr.
Denver, CO 80204
Work   (303) 573-5903
Fax   303573-0246
www.artistsonsantafe.com

Main Street Gallery
106 Main Street
Murphys, CA   95247
Work   (209) 728-1000
Fax   (209) 728-9797
www.themainstreetgallery.net

Mamaroneck Artist's Guild
2120 Boston Post Rd.
Larchmont, NY 10538
Work   (914) 834-1117

Mariposa Gallery
113 Romero NW
Albuquerque, NM 87104
Work   (888) 842-9097

Martha Schneider Gallery
230 Superior St.
Chicago, IL 60610
Work   (312) 988-4033

Masters Gallery
815 C-17th Ave., S.W.
Calgary, ALberta, Canada T2T 0A1
Work   (403) 245-2064
Fax   (403) 244-1636
www.mastersgalleryltd.com

Matrix Gallery
115 N. Main St.
Blacksburg, VA 24060
Work   (540) 951-3566

Miller Gallery
2715 Erie Ave.
Cincinnati, OH 45208
Fax   (513) 871-4429
www.miller-gallery.com

Mobilia Gallery
358 Huron Ave.
Cambridge, MA 02138
Work   (617) 876-2109
Fax   (617) 876-2110
mobilia-gallery.com

Mountain Top Gallery
Main St., P.O. Box 626
Windham, NY 12496
Work   (518) 734-3104

Museum Gallery at Schenectady Museum
15 Nott Terrace Hgts.
Schenectady, NY 12308
Work   (518) 382-7890

Nancy Shaw-Cramer Gallery
P.O. Box 26, 76 Main Street
Vineyard Haven, MA 02568
Work   (508) 696-7323

New Stone Age
9-8407 West Third St.
Los Angeles, CA 90048
Work   (323) 658-5969

Northern Clay Center
2424 Franklin Ave. E.
Minneapolis, MN 55406
Work   (612) 339-8007
Fax   (612) 339-0592
www.northernclaycenter.org

Northwest Craft Center
Seattle Center
Seattle, WA 98109
Work   (206) 728-1555

Object Art Atelier
111 Dawson St.
Philadelphia, PA 19127
Work   (215) 482-5681
Fax   (215) 483-8707

Orange County Museum of Art Museum Store
3333 Bristol St.
Costa Mesa, CA 92626
Work   (714) 662-3366
Fax   (714) 662-3818

Out of the Fire
100 Garfield Pkwy. #4
Bethany Beach, DE 19930

Palo Alto Art Center
1313 Newell Rd.
Palo Alto, CA 94303
Work   (650) 329-2366
Fax   (650) 326-6165

Peck Gallery
424 Wickenden St.
Providence, RI 02903
Work   (401) 751-0017

Penland Gallery
Penland School of Crafts
Penland, NC 28765
Work   (828) 765-6211

Phoenix Gallery
919 Massachusetts
Lawrence, KS 66044
Work   (785) 843-0080
Fax   (785) 841-0044
phoenixgallery.net

Pinch
179 Main Street
Northampton, MA 01060
Work   (413) 586-4509
Fax   (413) 586-4512

Portfolio Art Gallery
2007 Devine St.
Columbia, SC 29205
Work   (803) 256-2434

Prime Gallery
52 McCaul St.
Toronto, Ontario M5T 1V9, Canada
Work   (416) 593-5750
Fax   (416) 593-0942

Pryde's Old Westport
115 Westport Rd.
Kansas City, MO 64111
Work   (816) 531-5588

Raymond Avenue Gallery
761 Raymond Ave.
St. Paul, MN 55114
Work   (651) 644-9200

Red Star Studios Ceramics Center
821 West 17th St.
Kansas City, MO 64108
Work   (816) 474-7316

River Art Group Gallery
418 Villita Court, Suite 1400
San Antonio, TX 78205-2919
Work   (210) 226-8752

Robert F. Nichols
419 Canyon Rd.
Santa Fe, NM 87501
Work   (505) 982-2145
Fax   (505) 982-7171
robertnicholsgallery.com

Rochester Art Center
320 E. Center St.
Rochester, MN 55904
Work   (507) 282-8629
Fax   (507) 282-7737

Running Ridge Gallery
640 Canyon Road
Santa Fe, NM 87501
Work   (505) 988-2515
Fax   (505) 988-7692
runningridgegallery.com

Saint George Pottery
Route 131
St. George, ME 04857
Work   (207) 372-9671

Sansar
4805 Bethesda Ave.
Bethesda, MD 20814
Work   (301) 652-8676
Fax   (301) 652-8678

Santa Fe Pottery
323 S. Guadalupe St.
Santa Fe, NM 87501
Work   (505) 989-3363
Fax   (505) 989-3363
www.santafepottery.com

Sara Thomas Collection
5041 France Ave. So.
Minneapolis, MN 55410
Work   (612) 920-5033

Selo/Shevel Gallery
301 S. Main St.
Ann Arbor, MI 48104
Work   (734) 761-4620
Fax   (734) 761-4308
www.seloshevelgallery.com

Shaw Cramer Gallery
76 Main St.
Vineyard Haven, MA 02568
Work   (508) 696-7323

Show of Hands
2610 E. Third Ave.
Denver, CO 80206
Work   (303) 399-0201
Fax   (303) 321-2924
www.showofhandsdenver.com

Snyderman Gallery
303 Cherry St.
Philadelphia, PA 19106
Work   (215) 238-9576
Fax   (215) 238-9351
www.snyderman-works.com

Society For Contemporary Craft
2100 Smallman St.
Pittsburgh, PA 15222
Work   (412) 261-7003
Fax   (412) 261-1941
www.contemporarycraft.org

Solomon Dubnick Gallery
2131 Northrop Ave.
Sacramento, CA 95825
Work   (916) 920-4547
Fax   (916) 923-6356
www.sdgallery.com

Southwest Scholl of Art & Craft
300 Augusta
San Antonio, TX 78205
Work   (210) 224-1848
Fax   (210) 224-9337

St. George Pottery
HC 61, Box 162
St. George, ME 04857

Work   (207) 372-9671

Stoneware Gallery
778 Corydon Ave.
Winnepeg, Manitoba R3M 0Y1
Work   (204) 475-8088
Fax   (204) 452-8212

Supermud/Clay Hand Gallery
2744 Broadway, 2nd Floor
NYC, NY 10025

Symmetry Gallery
348 Broadway
Saratoga Springs, NY 12866
Work   (518) 584-5090

Teeks Gallery
On the Square
Wimberley, TX 78676
Work   (512) 847-8868

The American Gallery
6600 Sylvania Ave.
Sylvania, OH 43560
Work   (419) 882-8949

The Artful Hand Gallery
36 Copley Place @ 100 Huntington Ave.
Boston, MA 02116
Work   (617) 262-9601
Fax   (617) 262-0934

The Artistic Hand, Inc.
353 N. Central Ave.
Oviedo, FL 32765
Work   (407) 366-7882

The Biddle Gallery
2840 Biddle Ave.
Wyandotte, MI 48192
Work   (734) 281-4779
www.biddlegallery.com

The Clay Place
The Mineo Building
5416 Walnut St.
Pittsburgh, PA 15232
Work   (412) 682-3737
Fax   (412) 682-3239
wwwClayplace.com

The Clay Studio
139 N. 2nd St.
Philadelphia, PA 19123
Work   (215) 925-3453
Fax   (215) 925-7774
www.theclaystudio.org

The Collector
2067 Merrick Rd.
Merrick, NY 11566
Work   (516) 379-0805

The Company of Craftsmen
43 W. Main St.
Mystic, CT 06355
Work   (860) 536-4189

The Detroit Artist's Market
4719 Wood ward
Detroit , MI 48201
Work   (313) 832-8540
Fax   (313) 832-8543
detroitartists@juno.com

The Fisher Gallery
Farmington Valley Arts Center
25 Arts Center Lane
Avon, CT 06001
Work   (860) 678-1867
Fax   (860) 674-1877

The Gallery
109 E. 6th St.
Bloomington, IN 47408
Work   (812) 336-0564

The Guild Shop
118 Cumberland St.
Toronto, Ontario M5R 1A6
Work   (416) 921-1721
Fax   (416) 977-3552

The North Star/Anderson Gallery
307 West Green St.
Wilson , NC 27893
Work   (252) 237-6677
Fax   (252) 237-6632

The Signature Shop & Gallery
3267 Rosewell Road N.W.
Atlanta, GA 30305
Work   (404) 237-4426
www.thesignatureshop.com

The Society of Arts and Crafts
101 Arch St.
Boston, MA 02110
Work   (617) 345-0033
www.society of Crafts.org

The Source Fine Arts
4137 Pennsylvania
Kansas City, MO 64111
Work   (816) 931-8282
Fax   (816) 931-8283

The Sybaris Gallery
202 E. Third St.
Royal Oak, MI 48067
Fax   (248) 544-8101

The Works Gallery
303 Cherry St.
Philadelphia, PA 19106
Work   (215) 922-7775
Fax   (215) 238-9351
www.snyderman-works.com

Thornebrook Gallery
2441 NW 43rd St., Suite 6D
Gainsville, FL 32606
Work   (352) 378-4947

Toledo Museum of Art
The Collector's Corner
P.O.1013, Monrow St.
Toledo, OH 43697
Work   (419) 255-8000

Tower Cerlan Gallery
522 West Short St.
Lexington, KY 40507
Work   (859) 252-7284
Fax   (859) 252-4167

Trax
1306 3rd St.
Berkley, CA 94710
Work   (510) 526-3655
Fax   (510) 526-0279

Triology Gallery
120 E. Main St.
Nashville, IN 47448
Work   (812) 988-4030
Fax

Turman Gallery
107 W. Lawrence
Helena, MT 59601
Work   (406) 443-0340
Fax

Tuscan Pot Studio & Gallery
447 Water St.
Saugatuck, MI 49453
Work   (616) 857-6117

Twist
30 NW 23rd Place
Portland, OR 97210
Work   (503) 224-0334

Upcountry Connection Gallery
Mauna Kea Center
65-1190 Mamalahoa Hwy.
Kamuela, HI 96743
Work   (808) 885-0623
Fax   (808) 885-4366

Verdigris Gallery
The Cannery
2801 Leavenworth
San Francisco, CA 94133
Work   (415) 440-2898
www.verdigrisgallery.com

Wave Gallery
9 Whitney Ave.
New Haven, CT 06510
Work   (203) 624-3032

Winnipeg Art Gallery, Gallery Shop
300 Memorial Blvd.
Winnipeg, MAnitoba R3C 1V1 Canada
Fax   (204) 788-4998

World's Window
332 W. 63rd St.
Kansas City, MO 64113
Work   (816) 361-2500

Yeiser Art Center
200 Broadway
Paducah, KY 42001-0732
Work   (270) 442-2453

Bibliography

Cardozo, Sidney B., Masaaki, Hirano, eds. *Uncommon Clay.* Tokyo, Japan: Kodansha International Ltd., 1987.

Clark, Garth. *A Century of Ceramics in the United States; 1878-1978.* New York: E.P. Dutton, 1979.

———, *The Eccentric Teapot: Four Hundred Years of Invention.* New York: Abbeyville Publishing Group, 1989.

———, ed. *Ceramic Art: Commend and Review 1882-1977.* New York: E.P. Dutton, 1978.

de Waal, Edmund, *Bernard Leach: St Ives Artists.* London: Tate Gallery Publishing Ltd., n.d.

Frederick, Warren, ed. "The Politics of Pottery", *Ceramics Monthly.* Jan., 1987.

Gardner, Helen. *Art Through the Ages.* Rev. by Horst de la Croix & Richard G. Tansey.
New York: Harcourt Brace Jovanovich, Inc., 1975.

Halper, Vicki. *Clay Revisions: Plate, Cup, Vase.* Seattle: Seattle Art Museum, 1987.

Higby, Wayne. "Useful Pottery", *Ceramics Monthly.* April, 1986.

Illian, Clary. *A Potter's Workbook.* Iowa City: University of Iowa Press, 1999.

Lane, Peter. *Ceramic Form: Design & Decoration.* 2nd rev. ed., London: A&C Black Limited, 1998.

Leach, Bernard. *A Potter's Work,* Tokyo: Kodansha International Ltd., 1967.

———, Exhibition Catalog, N.p., 1966.

———, *Hamada: Potter.* Tokyo, Japan: Kodansha International Ltd., 1975.

———, *The Potter's Book.* Great Britain: Transatlantic Arts Inc., 1976.

———, *The Potter's Challenge.* ed. David Outerbridge U.S.A.: E.P. Dutton, 1975.

Lucie-Smith, Edward. *The Story of Craft: The Craftsman's Role in Society.* New York: Van Nostrand Reinhold Company Inc., 1981.

McTwigan, Michael. Essay from the exhibition catalog *Surface and Form: A Union of Polarities in Contemporary Ceramics.* N.p., n.d.

Moeran, Brian. "William Morris: The Arts and Crafts Aesthetic Pipeline", *Studio Potter.* Vol. 11, No. 2, 1983.

Randall, Ted. "Being and Meaning", *Ceramic Monthly.* Nov., 1984.

Rawson, Phillip, *Ceramics.* Philadelphia: University of Pennsylvania Press, 1984. (From *Ceramics* by Phillip Rawson. Copyright 1984 University of Pennsylvania Press. Reprinted with permission.)

Read, Herbert, *The Meaning of Art.* London: Faber & Faber, 1931.

Webb, Michael. Introduction to *Bernard Leach, Hamada & Their Circle.* Yeovil, UK: Marston House, 1992.

Whybrow, Marion. *The Leach Legacy: St Ives Pottery and its Influence.* Bristol: Sansom & Company, 1966.

Wright, Catherine, "The Bones of the Bowl", *Studio Potter.* Vol. 17, No. 1, 1988.

Yanagi, Soetsu. *The Unknown Craftsman.* Adapted by Bernard Leach. Tokyo, Japan, Kodansha International Ltd., 1972.